THE MAN WHO SHOT
THE GREAT WAR

The remarkable story of George Hackney – the Belfast soldier who took his camera to war

Mark Scott

Published 2016 by Colourpoint Books
an imprint of Colourpoint Creative Ltd
Colourpoint House, Jubilee Business Park
21 Jubilee Road, Newtownards, BT23 4YH
Tel: 028 9182 6339
Fax: 028 9182 1900
E-mail: sales@colourpoint.co.uk
Web: www.colourpoint.co.uk

First Edition
First Impression

Designed by April Sky Design, Newtownards
Tel: 028 9182 7195
Web: www.aprilsky.co.uk

Printed by W&G Baird Ltd, Antrim

ISBN 978-1-78073-095-0

About the author: Mark Scott is a photographer and recently taught the subject at Queen's University in Belfast. He also works as a researcher at the Royal Ulster Rifles Museum in Belfast. He was a research consultant in making the DoubleBand Films and BBC Northern Ireland production of the film documentary 'The Man Who Shot The Great War' which aired in November 2014, and on BBC2 nationwide in November 2016. He frequently tours France and Flanders photographing the landscapes of the old battlefields.

CONTENTS

The Memory Jar

As I sit thinking, the past returns,
Unbidden; with awful clarity
The lid comes off the memory jar.
A plurality of images emerge
Vying for supremacy. I focus on one;
Others clamour behind it, impatiently waiting their turn,
Like recalcitrant children.
Some memories would be best forgotten.
Deep repression eventually provides a springboard
To propel them foremost. Confronting sorrow and muffled pain
Recalls the past with cruel accuracy, but it must
Be countenanced, pain and hurt rekindled, before they
Can begin to ebb, assuaged, by being permitted fresh scrutiny.
I seek balance, and summon the next memory – a better one?
A happy one, to foil and balm the pain of its predecessor.
Life gives memories, and it also gives balance.
And there remains one certainty.
Once the lid comes off the memory jar,
It's impossible to replace it.

Patricia Fawcett

FOREWORD

The story of George Hackney, 'The Man Who Shot the Great War' is a journey. It begins in a time of relative innocence, a tumultuous time to be sure at the outbreak of the First World War and in the wake of the Irish Home Rule Crisis. The journey begins in Belfast, a city defiant against both the Government and Irish Nationalists, having created its own army, the Ulster Volunteer Force (UVF), including the Young Citizen Volunteers (YCV), and faced down any threat of Ulster being railroaded into an Irish nation divided from the United Kingdom. No modern soldier could imagine themselves into their shoes. We in the modern age are too calloused by war; we've seen it on TV in 3D and in the very games our children play. We are a people more cynical about killing and certainly towards concepts of King and country.

The people of the era were people of their time. Honest God-fearing folk tied together closely by their Protestant faith, sober and upright but with an optimistic, cheerful outlook and a warmth and generosity born of a wealthy, productive corner of the UK. My own grandfather was one of those Belfast people who had volunteered for the UVF and then, with the outbreak of war, volunteered for the King.

Often mistakenly called Kitchener volunteers, the vast majority had already enlisted ahead of the celebrated poster campaign by the field marshal, like my grandfather. He had settled his affairs, ensured my grandmother and her two toddlers – my uncles – were looked after and on the 11 August 1914, just over a week after war was declared, signed on for King and Ulster.

He signed on with his friends, young men of leisure and, much influenced by the humour of young men and the silent cowboy movies they adored, he gave his occupation as 'holder upper' on enlisting. This was a slanted reference to a Belfast character, a foreman in the shipyard of East Belfast, known by all and sundry as the 'sheriff'. If the hammering and banging of tools outside his office ever paused – even for a minute – he would run out shouting "Where's the hold up?" One of my grandfather's friends went one better and, when asked his religion by the recruiting sergeant, replied "ventriloquist". Without looking up, the orderly corporal filling in the ledger of recruits barked "Spell it!" They were innocents embarking on the most destructive, depraved and hideous war mankind has ever seen and with no idea what could lie ahead.

George Hackney had his camera to record the journey. With the opening photographs he lets us glimpse the men as they steam across the channel on their way to the front and to a time and place more different from the world they were leaving than any sane person could ever imagine and from which no man who made that short journey could never return. It must be hugely poignant for the author who sees his own great-grandfather in several of the photographs. The clarity of the images of Sergeant James Scott is striking. Pinpoint sharp, you can see the very character of Sergeant Scott in the image. What is fascinating is the faces of the men. Like Sergeant Scott, cheery and kind – it's in their eyes and their careless easy pose. It reminds me of the heady days of March 2003 ahead of the Liberation of Iraq. Goodwill towards all men abounded and the young men of the First Battalion of the Royal Irish Regiment I was leading across the border were optimistic, excited and feeling generous towards the Iraqis and all mankind and deferential and most respectful towards Islam and Muslims.

How that all changed and in the dark modern times where the beasts of the Death Cult called IS, Taliban, Whabbis and Deobandis have taken virtual ownership of Islam. Islam became a faith that, it would appear, will spill blood to avenge even a perceived slight against it, yet remains sullen and silent when innocents are slaughtered in the name of Islam. Where are the mullahs decrying this slaughter? Where are the marches of the ordinary Muslims to say "not in my name?" Amongst the military there is no longer the openness, blind trust and generosity; soldiers have learned to be wary of Muslims, understand their various paramilitary uniforms of blue burkas, black burkas, beards, long and short, with or without mustache. All the signs carry a code message and it is not "I love you!" Innocence was gone. For a while civilians mocked them, righteous actors condemned the lack of generosity towards refugees seeking to use the mayhem of the wars to swarm into Europe. And then came Paris of 13 November 2015 – Black Friday. The luvvies fell silent. We were all at war.

Soldiers like George went on a similar journey. For them it was the Kaiser's men, then the communists, then the Nazis. But for the vast majority it was not so for those on the home front in 1916. They remained in the idealistic world of Edwardian Britain.

George, like my grandfather, had joined with his friend,

the local minster's son. In George's case it was Paul Pollock, much younger than George. No doubt the older man felt protective towards the minister's boy. In my grandfather's case the young man, Robert McDermott, was his platoon commander, yet my grandfather, then 28 and an older man, must have also felt protectively towards the younger man. I can imagine my grandfather assuring Rev Dr McDermott, the man who had married him, that he would look out for young Robert. Both were to die tragically very early on in the campaign, Robert McDermott being the first officer from the famous Ulster Division to fall in the spring of 1915, Paul fated to be lost – literally – on the first day of the Somme.

For all of these young men the driving motivation was duty and loyalty as well as no doubt a great thirst for adventure. Mixed photos of landscapes and military subjects, the photos of 1915, maintain their innocence, but yet with increasingly alarming and ominous images.

The story now takes a deep turn. The images of the attack on the Somme on the 1 July 1916 and the aftermath is the turning point. The images are very different from here on. The faces are grim, the poses stiff and tense. The three pictures of the 1 July show a bombardment and rows of German prisoners. But they don't, as images, really allow us into the minds of the men who were there. Remember they were also seeing this for the first time. Trying to make sense of it. With hindsight we know that this is not possible – but they tried… and kept on trying, even as old men. When Paul Pollock, George's friend went missing, one of the thousands never found, George wrote to the minister and the letter he received in return was both poignant and in some respects naïve with the heavy 'duty to country' sentiments of the time. We can't know exactly what George made of it, but by now reading the letter from the other side of reality he must have been shaking his head, glad in some respects that Paul's father was still in that calm safe world where sacrifice was duty and not in the place where death was a cynical daily visitor who plundered without rhyme or reason at will, mocking any notion of death or glory with corruption and gore. They read about it in the papers. It was still far away.

George photographs the graves of the fallen – where there are graves to photograph – as if to bring home to the families some past trace of the loved one, some comfort. These were the last photos in the album. A fitting conclusion. Where was the glory? Where was the good? But we know from George's diaries that he is moving further away, deeper into the dark place where there is no innocence. His very faith is shaken.

We know that after the war George made a life for himself – a good life and living – and immersed once more in his Presbyterian faith and amongst his old colleagues, sought to allow healing to happen. For many it did. For him it did not. Why?

We can't really know but the clues are clear. George was allowed to carry a camera and photograph openly. This was most unusual indeed. Any other photos show landscapes that would interest a sniper – and some photos showed snipers. It dawns; clearly George had been a sniper. And now it all begins to make sense. George was not fleeing from what the war had done. It was what he had done. From here we continue on a journey which I could never on one hand have guessed, yet on the other hand the final twist, which you must read on in order to discover, did not surprise me in the least. In the modern age we have a name for George's suffering: Post Traumatic Stress Disorder PTSD. In George's time there was no recognition or treatment for PTSD. This was an age when they still shot those considered to be cowards.

I don't believe it is for us to judge down through the years and across people and beliefs we could never conjure up again. George's journey is a glimpse. If one watches it carefully one can get an attenuated idea of what that journey was like. It is a journey from the certainty of empire and faith, to the very bowels of hell and hopelessness. It is a journey very well worth following Mark Scott on as he takes us along George's journey. But remember – many young men and women amongst us now are on that journey. If nothing else, I hope reading *The Man Who Shot The Great War* will help you in some small way to understand.

Colonel Tim Collins, OBE
2016

Knob to release glides
(missing)

Button to release baseboard.

rings for sling strap.

Diaphragm numbers &
pointer

side struts

Shutter release

focussing scale

focussing lever

Knobs for drawing front out
Left hand knob moves a little
to the right to allow of front
being released to close camera)

INTRODUCTION

At Townhall Street in Belfast on the 14 September 1914 a group of around 700 young men, all members of an organisation called the Young Citizen Volunteers, enlisted en masse in the British Army to fight in the war against Germany. On enlistment they formed the 14th Battalion of the Royal Irish Rifles, and became part of the 36th (Ulster) Division. These young men came from all walks of life and all religious backgrounds. From its inception as a civilian organisation in 1912 the aim of the Young Citizen Volunteers (YCV) had been to become non-sectarian and non-political, setting them apart from the Ulster Volunteer Force regiments that had formed around that time in opposition to the threat of the imposition of Home Rule by the Westminster government. As a fighting battalion they proudly maintained their individuality by retaining their unique insignia and shoulder titles. Although they were officially the 14th Battalion of the Royal Irish Rifles they became known simply as the YCV.

Notwithstanding their predominantly Protestant make up, the membership was drawn from other religious backgrounds and a wide geographical base; many were well educated young men with skills reflective of the trades and professions prevalent in Ulster at that time. It is fair to say that this battalion contained more than its fair share of thinking men. This is evidenced by the numbers of diaries, drawings, pieces of poetry and memorabilia attributable to its members and held today in the archives of the Royal Ulster Rifles museum in Belfast, far more than is represented by the other Rifles battalions. Often ridiculed at the time for their individual standpoint, the YCV nevertheless proved themselves in the ferocious battles of the First World War, earning with pride their place in Ulster history.

One man, a corporal in the YCV battalion, showed exceptional forward thinking. He used skills learnt during the pre-war years to document the war using the relatively new medium of photography. George Hackney, contrary to military law at the time, brought a camera from Ireland to England and then on to France and Belgium and recorded his observations and experiences on film or glass plate negative. Through his photography we can see the periods of training, the daily rigours of life in the front lines, the horror of battle and the aftermath of death and destruction.

By recording his own experiences he immortalised the journey of his battalion and indeed the journey of the 36th Ulster Division. His photography is eerily reminiscent of much later work by photographers such as Robert Capa with his D-Day battle scenes and Tim Heatherington in his 'Restrepo' series taken recently in Afghanistan before his untimely death in Libya. One important difference was Hackney's 'access' to his subject. He was not 'embedded' with a group of soldiers, observing from arms length, perhaps kept in a safe location and shown what to photograph. Rather he was first and foremost a soldier himself, exposed to the same dangers as the men next to him and the men he photographed. It was not a case of George being in a dangerous situation but carrying on regardless; that was not how it was. As far as time and place were concerned he had little choice in the matter; he was a soldier of the King and was accordingly duty bound to follow orders and go where he was sent. He experienced the rigours and hardship of trench life at the same time and in the same locations as his friends in the YCV. He quickly learnt how to adapt with them and how to survive with them and indeed, ultimately, he learnt how to live with losing those same friends when they became casualties of war. What set him apart was that as an infantry soldier he took the extra step in deciding to use his knowledge and apply his skills to photograph all that he could to record his experiences forever.

Through the making of the BBC 1 Northern Ireland film documentary, 'The Man Who Shot The Great War' the author found himself in the privileged position of being able to research George Hackney's work. He was honoured to be given his own access to retrace the movements of this brave group of men through the unique photography of George Hackney, for in doing so he was retracing the footsteps of his own great-grandfather, Company Sergeant Major Jimmy Scott, a non-commissioned officer in the YCV battalion and for two years, George Hackney's sergeant. George took several photographs of Jimmy Scott, photographs that were eventually handed on to Jimmy's widow, Jane, after he was killed in action near Messines in January 1917. The photographs that George took have now been in the Scott family for a full century. In the years since George first captured them the images of Jimmy Scott have been frozen and preserved. Four generations of the Scott family have proudly looked Jimmy in the eye through George's lens, able to make up their own minds as to the sort of man he was, and to put a face to the name on a grave. Such is the power of photography.

Wherever possible George's photographs have been studied alongside his own notes and the information in those notes has been corroborated using the official battalion war diaries and orders, in conjunction with information taken from the personal diaries of men from the same battalion. In a number of instances corroboration comes in the form of the author's own photographs, taken from almost the exact position from which George took the original shots. The identities of those men shown in the photographs have been established by studying George's own index of names, alongside whenever possible, archive battalion photographs of the day. It is the author's sincere wish that someone reading this work can identify for the first time a distant relative so that another face can be put to a name carved in cold stone in some French or Belgian cemetery or memorial.

The question of George Hackney's role as a soldier has come up many times during research. His photographs hint at him having a specialist role in the YCV battalion and there is strong evidence, all be it circumstantial, that he was most likely a member of the scout/sniper section.

The battalion scouts, or Permanent Patrol as they were known, operated in No-Man's-Land close to the enemy positions, watching and listening and feeding back information to battalion intelligence officers for analysis and further action. Within their number were the snipers and their observers or spotters. The snipers, masters of camouflage and covert movement, made their way into their own carefully sited and constructed hides where they waited, unseen, often for hours on end for an enemy target to present itself. When the moment came the sniper would dispatch the target with a ruthless, cold, efficiency aided by a smooth trigger action and steady hand.

The snipers were unpopular, even amongst some of their own men, who thought them to be a 'dirty' and un-gentlemanly weapon, even in that dirtiest of wars. The psychological effect of sniper fire on the enemy could be devastating. Just one well placed and concealed sniper could have a massive effect on operations in the area in which he was operating, though the sniper himself also suffered. Even when the infantrymen of a battalion were taking their turn in the line there were times when they could relax, to a certain extent. However the sniper was constantly engaging the enemy from his lonely hide, living under constant stress and always fearing that he himself had become the target and was being lined up in the crosshairs of his counterpart's scope. If captured by an enemy scouting patrol a sniper could expect nothing less than death, such was the strength of feeling against him. For this reason many snipers, and also scouts, removed the fleur-de-lis insignia, which they were entitled to wear, from their uniforms.

Small clues to support the proposition that George was a scout or sniper can be drawn from his own photographs. For instance, a particular older model of rifle, which may be his own, can be seen in the foreground of some of his trench images, suggesting that he may have had to prop the weapon against the trench wall in order to operate his camera. The strongest clue is, as we can see clearly, that he could operate his camera in view of senior officers, and indeed take pictures of them. If George was a battalion scout, and many of his photographs put him in the company of men who were known to be scouts, then his photography would have been a valuable intelligence asset to a forward thinking battalion commander, his landscapes of German trench lines bringing the available trench maps to life with an up-to-date clarity.

There is however no official record that gives his specific role. At the end of the day, a century later, it matters little. What we do know is that George, like countless others, did not leave the battlefield unscathed; he was affected by his time at the front. His experiences lived with him for decades after the war had ended, and were very probably one of the factors at play when he appeared to question his own life and beliefs in his twilight years. What matters is that regardless of his role, George Hackney chose to bring his camera to war. In doing so he left us a fascinating and vivid record of a life that many men chose to forget. He leaves us with photo-documentary work, worthy of the finest war photographers, depicting a man's journey from book-seller to soldier, from Belfast in 1914 to the hell of France and Belgium in 1916. Most importantly we can now put names and some details of their lives to those men whose faces gaze back at us from his photographs of a century ago. He preserved their images in remembrance, frozen in time and place at the release of a shutter, when the images and memories of so many others were lost forever, like tears in the rain.

WHO WAS THIS MAN?

George Naphtali Hackney was born on the 12 August 1888 in Belfast. He was the youngest of a family of five children having one older brother and three older sisters. His father was a book keeper who worked for the Finlay Mineral Water Company and the family initially lived at 24 Manor Street in North Belfast before moving to Hopefield Avenue and then to Lansdowne Road in 1915.

The Hackney family were Presbyterians and regularly attended St Enoch's Presbyterian Church at the Carlisle Circus junction in Belfast where the Antrim Road meets the Crumlin Road. St Enoch's Church played an important part in George's teenage years and early adulthood. He was a member of the Boys' Brigade and had made friends with other young men amongst the congregation who, like him, joined the ranks of the Young Citizen Volunteers and eventually the 14th Battalion Royal Irish Rifles. One notable fellow recruit was Paul Pollock, son of the minister at St Enoch's, the Reverend Alexander Pollock.

In his early twenties George was employed in an evangelical bookshop at Fisherwick Place in Belfast where he became an avid reader of the various religious books. He also helped his sister, Jenny, manage her florist's shop and it was around this time that he became interested in both photography and the outdoor life. He learnt his photographic skills from a fellow member of the congregation at St Enoch's, a man called Ernie McClatchey from 234 Spamount Street in Belfast. Ernie had been involved with organising the Boys' Brigade in the church and undoubtedly knew George from his time growing up in the Brigade.

From perhaps as early as 1912 George was interested in photography, a subject which went hand in hand with another of his favourite pastimes, rambling. He became involved with the Co-Operative Holiday Association (CHA) which was an organisation established at the end of the nineteenth century to give working-class people access to affordable and organised educational holidays. These holidays were typically of one week's duration and incorporated often strenuous daily rambles in rural areas. The CHA encouraged its members to take part in cultural activities such as recitals, lectures and concerts during the evenings, often following a hard day's walk. George participated enthusiastically in a number of these holidays in the Lake District, the Isle of Man and also closer to home in counties Fermanagh and Donegal. He struck up friendships with a number of people whom he met during the CHA holidays and continued to correspond with these friends long after the holidays had ended and into the war years.

One young lady who continued to write to George was Doris Heyhoe. Her correspondence gives us an insight into the changes taking place as war broke out and how they impacted on everyday life.

Doris lived in the White Hart Hotel in Grimsby, which still exists today. At one point it was owned or managed by her father but later passed into the hands of her grandmother. Although she lived on the premises Doris did not work there, she worked in a stationery shop nearby. The available correspondence between Doris and George, is unfortunately one way as the letters he sent to her no longer exist. However it gives some sense of the background to the period leading up to and including the outbreak of war. In 1912 she began studying German at evening classes after work. At the same time she makes her feeling clear about George having begun a course in Chemistry, something which no doubt was to assist in the developing of his photographs. In June of that year Doris wrote:

"Now I'm going to talk to you like a sister. I think you're a silly old ass to start with your Chemistry classes during the summer months, don't you get enough of it in the winter? You'll go and undo all the good your holiday has done for you. If you have any spare time you should spend it playing tennis or walking, it would do you a jolly sight more good than sticking in a stuffy laboratory, why you'll be nothing but a washed out nag by Christmas. I really think it very foolish of you."

Later, in September 1912 she began her own studies:

"Our evening classes commenced last week, I'm studying German. I have one or two German friends in the town which makes it a little more interesting."

As the months passed by Doris continued to write to George. By September 1912 in Belfast George had joined the newly formed Young Citizen Volunteers. He continued to participate in the CHA holidays and met Doris and her friend Edith Brader on a number of occasions, visiting Belleek and Bundoran.

In her letters to George Doris commented on many of the historical events taking place during those turbulent pre-war years. In one letter, undated but most likely written before April 1913, she informs George of her latest holiday plans for the coming summer and makes mention of the following:

"I'm glad the Suffragettes are giving you a pretty lively time, it will at any rate rouse your interest in the movement and I'm afraid you will probably have a livelier time later on."

On the 11 August 1914, just after the outbreak of war, Doris once again wrote to George obviously in response to a postcard that she had previously received from him:

"Are you volunteering for active service that you are so pessimistic? I got your card today and note you are still at home so am writing at once.
Grimsby is one mass of soldiers. Every available spot has been turned into barracks. Our house is accommodating 17 men and about the same number of horses. We have on average six aeroplanes over daily.
Saturday night things were very serious, 13,000 troops were at Cleethorpes, most of them regulars who had been hastily summonsed from Manchester

etc without the knowledge of the town, the whole of the foreshore was full from end to end with troops fully armed, everyone was of course cleared off the promenade and pier at about 8 o'clock. Spurn Lighthouse light was extinguished and one of the soldiers told me afterwards that nearly the whole of the home fleet was in the North Sea until 3 o'clock on the Sunday morning. They were quite ready for an attack which thank God did not take place but we are in a very dangerous spot just here if the German Navy happens to come out of the Kiel Canal.

Things seem to be all in favour of those plucky little Belgians and I think there is no chance of them doing anything else but winning. It seems to be the Kaiser against the World as far as I can see and I don't think he can do anything else but get the hiding of his life. I feel so sorry for the German people I don't think they wished to war with England in the least – but here it is.

Business is absolutely at a standstill as our men are working half time and of course the fishing is absolutely stopped. Next week will see all the trawlers laid up with the exception of 40 or so which are sweeping the North Sea for mines.

I just left this letter (it's 9 o'clock) to see a party consisting of about 60 men and the same number of horses and about a doz wagons going to Immingham by road, about 11 miles. I guess the poor fellows will be done by the time they arrive.

The public houses and clubs here have orders to close 9.45 prompt. Hurrah!"

Meantime back in Belfast, George and the other members of the Young Citizen Volunteers had, only weeks earlier, joined with the Ulster Volunteer Force regiments in arming themselves in opposition to imposition of the Home Rule Bill. On the 10 July 1914 Sir Edward Carson and the Ulster Unionist Council met to lay down plans for their Ulster Provisional Government. In response King George V himself had convened meetings in London in an attempt to relieve the tensions building in Ulster.

On the 4 August everything changed. War had been declared and the loyalties of the Ulstermen fell once more to King and Country against the common foe, Germany.

For Doris one question still remained and this most likely set the tone of her next letter – was George volunteering for active service? In the letter, dated the 20 August 1914 Doris re-enforced her question:

"Is anything definite being done yet with your Corps of Volunteers? Am awaiting anxiously any news of what you are doing over there."

In reality quite a bit had been done. Sir Edward Carson had obtained an assurance from Lord Kitchener, the Minister for War, that the Ulster Volunteer Force regiments, and the Young Citizen Volunteers, could form their own 'Ulster' Division. On the 14 September George and his Young Citizen friends effectively became soldiers of the 14th Battalion, The Royal Irish Rifles. Made up of this and other units, the 36th (Ulster) Division had been born.

In her letter of the 21 October 1914 Doris revealed her knowledge of George's move to Finner Camp at Bundoran in County Donegal, ironically back to the same place where they had been on a CHA holiday together:

"Glad to have a line from you at last. I just had a short note saying you'd had orders to go to Finner – that was all. It's good to hear you're having a grand time, some poor fellows are having to work very hard and lead beds to sleep on after that…

…We still have 5000 troops about 6 miles from here and a few more thousand dotted about in various places.

Quite a big 'Chums' battalion of clerks etc has been formed here. They are to have navy blue uniforms as the stock of khaki has given out so they'll look nuts won't they?

I had a letter from my friend in S. Africa. He says every able bodied man there is drilling and by all accounts they've been these last few weeks.

I wonder when all the pandemonium will end. I do hope right soon. The stories that trickle through are horrible, poor fellows, it is a shame that life should be taken like that and poor beggars shot to pieces."

At Finner George had begun his basic military training. His previous knowledge of the area gave him a slight advantage over the other Belfast men in the battalion. He had previously stayed with a family called Gallagher in Bundoran during his CHA stays there. He called frequently with them during his training and was afforded some of the comforts of home. The accommodation at Finner consisted of eight-man tents and with winter drawing in the conditions became harsh.

In December 1914 the battalion took over the nearby Great Northern Railway Hotel and the men were billeted under its roof. Doris remarked on this development:

"Your letter was very interesting; you must be feeling very fit by now and quite swanky putting up at the best Hotel in Bundoran. Give my love to the Gallaghers when you see them next."

In January 1915 the battalion moved to a new, purpose built training camp at Randalstown in County Antrim. The recruits continued with their basic training and carried out route marches to training areas at Ballyscullion and Drumadarragh along with a recruiting march through Ballymena.

As time went on George kept up his correspondence with Doris Heyhoe. He also continued to receive advice and instruction on photography from Ernie McClatchey as well as updates on members of St Enochs Church who were already serving at the front.

It was during this period that George purchased the camera he would eventually take with him to France and Belgium. Ernie had sourced it from a dealer called Millar in Belfast. It was a second hand 'Watch Pocket' Klimax model which produced a print measuring 2½ inches by 1¾ inches. The camera was posted to George at Randalstown on approval and he agreed to buy it after a short trial period. Ernie McClatchey sent George a comprehensive hand written set of instructions along with a detailed and accurate diagram of the camera as, being second hand, the original manufacturers instruction manual had been lost. The 'Watch Pocket' camera was the ideal model for the job that George had in mind. Although a bellows style camera, it could be easily and quickly collapsed and folded up. In its folded state the camera measured just over six inches long by three inches wide and one and a quarter inches deep. It could easily fit into a military tunic pocket or a webbing pouch and could be made ready to take a photograph in a matter of seconds.

During his time at Randalstown George taught himself how to operate the new camera and sent a series of negatives to Ernie for development. Ernie returned the processed images with comment and criticism allowing George to quickly identify his mistakes and perfect his technique. During these early months of basic training George established the relationships with his senior officers and non-commissioned officers that would eventually lead to him being given unofficial 'access' to photograph the men of the YCV battalion during training and later during combat. A number of his early photographs show sergeants relaxing on their bunks. The sergeants' quarters were generally off limits to lower ranks and these particular photographs show that George was building up a level of trust with the men in the battalion who could influence the officers to allow him to continue with his photography.

One man who George photographed during the early days in training was Sergeant Jimmy Scott, a sergeant in 'B' Company, George's own company. He had previously served as a professional soldier with the 2nd Battalion, Royal Irish Fusiliers and was a veteran of the 1899–1902 Boer War. He was one of only a handful of experienced soldiers in the YCV battalion at that time and as such would have been held in high regard by the officers and men alike. It is no surprise that an intelligent, thinking man such as George should befriend a man from whom he could glean valuable knowledge which would help him to survive the ordeals of war.

George was also photographed (overleaf, front row forth from right) along with Jimmy Scott on the 17 March 1915 at Randalstown. The photograph is significant not just for

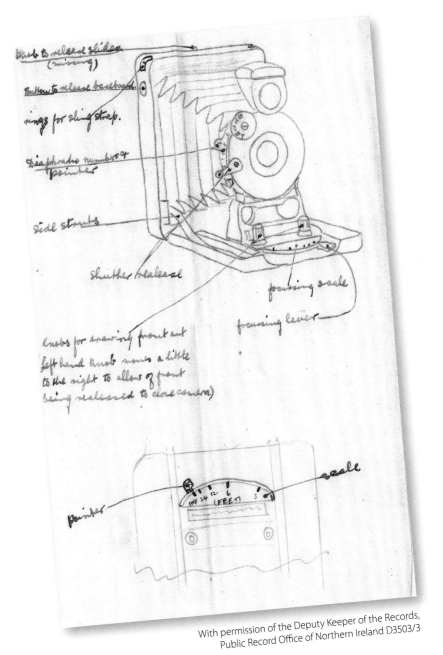

With permission of the Deputy Keeper of the Records, Public Record Office of Northern Ireland D3503/3

Courtesy of
the Royal
Ulster Rifles
Museum.

but for the context in which the photograph was taken. On close inspection it can be seen that Sergeant Scott is distributing shamrock to the men to be worn in their head-dress. The occasion would have been an important one for him as he had fought in the battle at Pieters Hill in South Africa after which Queen Victoria sent a telegraph to her troops containing the following message:

"I have heard with deepest concern of the heavy losses sustained by my brave Irish soldiers.

Her Majesty, the Queen, is pleased to order that in future, upon St Patrick's Day, all ranks of her Irish regiments shall wear, as a distinction, a sprig of shamrock in their head-dress to commemorate the gallantry of her Irish soldiers during the recent battles in South Africa."

George took three photographs of Jimmy Scott during training, two during their time at Randalstown and one at Seaford in East Sussex. The first of these photographs shows Jimmy relaxing on his bunk in his billet at Randalstown. He was obviously aware that the photograph was being taken as he lay reading a copy of the *Daily Sketch* newspaper. His rifle, early 'territorial pattern' leather belt and accoutrements can be seen hanging on the wall above him along with photographs of his wife, Jane and daughter Sadie. His collection of 'Players' cigarette cards can also be seen pinned along the shelf and wall of his private space.

The second photograph shows the men of 'B' Company resting during a route march in County Antrim. In this photograph we can see that the men have been issued with a number of different models of rifle including Lee Metford, 'Long' Lee Enfield and Lee Enfield rifles. They had not yet been issued with a modern standard weapon. In this photograph Jimmy Scott (second from left) appears to have been caught off-guard by George and looks to be feeling all of his 33 years, exhausted after the march.

The third (overleaf), and perhaps most striking photograph of Jimmy was taken after the YCV battalion moved to England for the final stages of their training before deploying to France. Here we see him mounted and carrying a Short Magazine Lee Enfield rifle (SMLE) in a pose that obviously harks back to his Boer War service when he was attached to a mounted infantry unit during the later stages of the campaign. In this photograph he was most likely using the horse in a supervisory role while the men were training on the rifle ranges.

The YCV battalion trained at Seaford between the 7 July–4 September 1915. The men generally

This page and overleaf: Courtesy the Scott family

enjoyed their stay during this period and often took outings to Eastbourne and Brighton at weekends. Their final month in England was spent at Bramshot camp where the men were issued with their modern SMLE rifles, latest pattern webbing and field service boots.

On the 1 October George had his own photograph taken along with his platoon and company. These were formed into a small album, a copy of which could be ordered by the men for two shillings and sixpence. He then packed his belongings and equipment which consisted of the following (as recorded by himself):

"One uniform, 2 shirts, 2 pr drawers, 1 blanket, 3 pr socks, 1 pr boots, cap comforter, Cap, Cardigan, Respirator, First Field Dressing, Ampoule of Iodine, Towel, Ground Sheet. My private property, in addition to this, was composed of watchpkt Klimax Camera, 12 sheaths, 8 doz plates, changing bag, photo-record book, flash-lamp, watch, 2 body belts, ink and pens, bottle ginger, shoes."

He turned in to bed at 11.20 pm and rose the following day for morning parade at 7.00 am. During the parade Lieutenant Mayes approached George and said something to him that he didn't immediately understand. George recorded the conversation as follows:

"Lieut. Mayes spoke to me and said, 'Are you getting your shivering on'? I begged his pardon and he repeated it but I could not understand him. He again repeated it and I wondered should I say 'yes' and try to find out afterwards from someone what he wanted. However, I just gave him a blank stare and he came to the conclusion that I did not understand him and he then said 'Did you not know you had been made a Lance Corporal'? I said 'No' and he then told me it had appeared in orders last night and to get my chevron on this evening sure. The news came as quite a surprise – I can't say I was pleased at the news, as I wasn't, and I thought it hardly fair to give anyone a stripe the day before leaving, but such are the ways of the Army."

He was then issued with his army paybook which contained his orders from Field Marshal Kitchener:

"You are ordered abroad as a soldier of the King to help our French comrades against the invasion of a common enemy. You have to perform a task which will need your courage, your energy, your patience.

Remember that the honour of the British Army depends upon your individual conduct. It will be your duty not only to set an example of discipline and perfect steadiness under fire but also to maintain the most friendly relations with those whom you are helping in this struggle. The operation in which you are engaged will, for the most part, take place in a friendly country and you can do your own country no better service than in showing yourself in France and Belgium in the true character of a British soldier. Be invariably courteous, considerate and kind. Never do anything likely to injure or destroy property and always look upon looting as a disgraceful act. You are sure to be met with a welcome and be trusted; your conduct must justify that welcome and that trust.

Your duty cannot be done unless your health is sound. So keep constantly on your guard against any excesses. In this new experience you might find temptations both in wine and women. You must entirely resist both temptations and, while treating women with perfect courtesy, you should avoid any intimacy.

Do your duty bravely.
Fear God.
Honour the King"

On the 3 October 1915 the men of the 14th Battalion, The Royal Irish Rifles, the YCV, paraded at 12 noon. They were each issued with 120 rounds of .303 calibre ammunition and marched to Liphook railway station to begin their journey to France. They were no longer the tram conductors or clerks, mill workers or fitters, teachers or lawyers that they were a year before. They were now fully trained soldiers of the King. In George's own words,

"Thus commenced our final act in the drama of the Great War".

FROM THE COAST TO THE FRONT

The first photograph in George Hackney's France album is entitled "Thoughts of Home". It is a strikingly well composed shot showing a young soldier alone with his thoughts on the deck of what must be the SS *Connaught* en route from Dublin to Holyhead on Tuesday 6 July 1915. It is strange that this photograph was included in the France album as the SS *Connaught* only ferried troops from Ireland to Great Britain. It was some two months before they finally set off for France on the paddle steamer, *Empress Queen*, a journey which took place during the hours of darkness to avoid detection by enemy submarines.

The soldier pictured can now be identified as Rifleman James Maxwell, No 6378 from 26 Bangor Street in Belfast. At the time the photograph was taken on the 6 July 1915 James Maxwell had good reason to be deep in thought – he had enlisted underage. In the 1911 Census which was taken on the 2 April, he was recorded as being twelve years of age, so at the time this photograph was taken he was only sixteen. Two of his older brothers had already joined the colours and were serving with the 8th Royal Irish Rifles and the 2nd Royal Irish Fusiliers.

James was a member of 'C' Company of the 14th Royal Irish Rifles. He continued to France with the battalion and served with his company right up to the battle at Thiepval on the 1 July 1916. Still underage, he took part in the great battle and was wounded. For sixteen days his whereabouts were unknown and the battalion had recorded him as being "missing in action". On the 3 July 1916 he was discovered with the 110th Field Ambulance unit, from where he was eventually evacuated to the base hospital, at which point his battalion was informed of his survival. It was then that his real age was finally discovered and he was not permitted to rejoin the battalion until over a year later on the 27 July 1917. On his return he would have received a warm welcome back in the ranks as a YCV man and Somme veteran, a rare 'original' replacement amongst the ever increasing number of English conscripts filling the gaps in the battalion.

By July 1917 the Young Citizens were operating in the Ypres sector in Belgium and involved in the final stages of preparation for what was to be known as the Third Battle of Ypres or the Battle of Langemark.

On the 16 August 1917, then of full military age, James Maxwell once again went 'over the top' with his battalion alongside the few remaining original Young Citizen Volunteers. On that day he was again wounded and was evacuated to base for the last time on the 31 August 1917. James survived the war along with his two brothers Samuel and John.

Having crossed to France on the *Empress Queen* the YCV battalion disembarked at Le Havre at 1.15 am on the morning of the 5 October 1915. They then travelled by rail through Rouen to Amiens where they marched north through the darkness to their first billets in the small village of Poulainville. Here, for the next two and a half weeks the Ulstermen experienced their first taste of French life as they were billeted in local homes, sheds and barns around the village.

Initially, on that first October night their billeting arrangements were quite chaotic. The officers and men, fatigued from their railway journey and march, struggled with both the darkness and the French language. Daylight revealed that there was room for improvement so the billets were re-organised in a way that assisted in the command of the battalion. Platoons and sections were assigned accommodation close together whenever possible to ease communication and movement. George Hackney and many of the men of 'B' Company found themselves billeted on Rue Irenee Defleselle which leads out from the church at the centre of the village roughly in the direction of nearby Bertangles until it meets the modern Route National N25. George took photographs of the billets in Poulainville, his first French village. The image opposite shows a group of six men posing along with the owner of the house. The battalion bombing instructor, Sergeant John Hunter can be seen standing second from left with John Ewing, George Hackney's friend, standing second from right.

John Hunter lived at 79 Northumberland Street in Belfast with his aunt. On joining the 14th Royal Irish Rifles he was appointed a Corporal in 'B' Company and then quickly promoted to Lance Sergeant, a term given to a man of Corporal rank who was 'acting' Sergeant. He was formally promoted to the rank of Sergeant just days after this photograph was taken on the 29 October 1915. Sergeant Hunter was a 'First Class' bomber and took the lead in training the bombers of the battalion in the various grenades in use at that time, including those used by German and French forces. On the 27 November 1915 he was transferred to 'C' Company where one of the men under his charge was Rifleman William 'Billy' McFadzean, also a 'C' Company bomber.

On the morning of 1 July 1916, just before the attack at Thiepval Wood two grenades fell from a box and had their pins dislodged among a group of men, which included Billy McFadzean, who were gathering in an assembly trench. From the training he had received and his knowledge of the killing power of the Mills Grenade, Billy would have instantly recognised that to do nothing in this situation would mean that very shortly he and many of those around him would be killed or very seriously injured.

In an act of supreme self sacrifice he threw himself on top of the two grenades in order to save the lives of those around him, knowing that for himself the outcome would ultimately be the same, he would die. For his action that morning Rifleman Billy McFadzean was posthumously awarded the Victoria Cross.

Recognition must be given to the level of training and instruction provided by John Hunter. There can be little doubt that this training played a part in prompting Billy's decisions and actions during the four long seconds before the detonation of the grenades which took his life that morning.

After the chaos and disruption of the battle neither William McFadzean's nor John Hunter's bodies could be found. The name of Rifleman William McFadzean, number 18278 was eventually carved onto the Thiepval Memorial to the Missing along with 72,192 other names.

Sergeant John Edward Hunter, number 14948 was recorded in the battalion records as first being wounded at some time on the 1 July 1916, then killed in action before finally being reported missing on the same date. By some administrative error his death was mistakenly recorded as taking place on the 1 September 1916 which was in all likelihood the acceptance date of his death for pension purposes. His name was not however carved on the Thiepval Memorial in France but can today be found on the Menin Gate Memorial to the Missing at Ypres in Belgium.

Once the battalion was billeted, a syllabus of training commenced, one aspect of which was the function and use of gas helmets. The use of various types of poisonous gas by both sides had by this time become a fact of war and the men had to be trained to use the equipment available to them to counter the effects of the gas, either deployed by the enemy or by their own forces and blown their direction on an ill wind. On the 17 October 1915 they were marched from their billets in Poulainville to a makeshift parade ground on the edge of the village. Here a trench had been dug which was filled with tear gas for training purposes. The men formed up in lines and after fitting their gas helmets, filed through the trench to test the helmets as well as to familiarise themselves with the equipment and its use in a poisonous environment. Some of the men complained of suffering from headaches afterwards and were excused training for the remainder of the day.

This image above is named "Bread Delivery, Poulainville". It was taken on Rue Irenee Defleselle. The exact location was identified by the author and the scene photographed today. The village pond has been filled in and replaced by a road junction but the view towards the church is essentially the same as when George took his photograph. It is likely that George stepped from the doorway of his billet to take the photograph of the bread cart as it approached him. Just to the right of the frame we can see two properties which were used to billet members of 'B' Company back in 1915. One of these is shown in the photograph on page 26. Today one of these properties has been re-built and the other extended upwards. Details of the original brickwork can still be seen.

On the 21 October 1915 the battalion received urgent orders to move from Poulainville to new billets at Beauval just south of Doullens. Before taking up their new billets however they joined up with the other battalions that formed the 109th Brigade along with those of the 107th Brigade. The two brigades, consisting entirely of Ulstermen then carried out a mock attack with the village of La Vicogne as the objective.

George wrote in his diary:

"Thurs 21st
Rose at 5.30 am and had breakfast at 6.30, parading at 7.30 and marching off at 8.00. A heavy mist was over the whole country so we were not able to see round us. We marched till 10.00 when the Brigade assembled and the Brigadier opened his orders and we commenced a manoeuvre over the country, advancing first in column then in formation for under artillery fire and finally in extended order, the operations ending at 1.30 pm when we formed up for dinner which consisted of beef soup – only. We then started off again and marched till 6 pm when we reached Beauval, where we billeted for the night, with the possibility of remaining till Monday."

George photographed a group of men resting "During Manoeuvres". They are carrying full packs but have not yet been issued with their steel 'Brodie' helmets. This photograph may have been taken along the road between Poulainville and La Vicogne, en route to Beauval.

On completion of their manoeuvres the Young Citizens marched off to their next billets in the village of Beauval. Here they made preparations and purchased supplies for their first tour of duty in the trenches. George walked around the town with John Hunter, the bombing sergeant and they bought candles for use in the trenches along with "a few odds and ends" from a branch of the Co-Operative Society which had been established in the town. The men of 'B' Company were billeted in French houses along Rue du Château d'Eau which led roughly west from the centre of the town.

George took a photograph, again a view from outside his billet which shows the village of Beauval from the Rue du Château d'Eau with two of his colleagues, unfortunately un-named, making their way towards him. One of these

men has a tin which he has thrown into the air. George captured the shot with the tin in mid air above his hand. He described this scene in his album as "happy men".

The author visited Beauval and was able to find the spot where George had stood to take the photograph. Remarkably the scene has changed very little in one hundred years.

The village is significant for a number of reasons relevant to the Young Citizens. Their stay in Beauval marked a turning point for the battalion. At that time they were finally trained to a level where they could take up positions in the front line. The Young Citizens had finally come of age and their next move would take them to the trenches. Beauval also marks the final resting place of the first of their number to die while in France.

During their spell in the front line trenches Rifleman William Lorimer from 106 Mountcollyer Avenue in Belfast, took ill with pneumonia. He was taken to No 4 Casualty Clearing Station (CCS) which at that time was based in the village but, unfortunately he passed away on the 13 November 1915 at twenty-four years of age leaving a widow, Mary Jane. He was buried in Beauval Communal Cemetery just behind the Cathedral, at that time the twenty-ninth British serviceman to be buried there. The cemetery would go on to be the final resting place for another two hundred and twenty British servicemen from the First World War and one Royal Canadian Air Force pilot killed in action in 1943 during the Second World War.

At the time of William Lorimer's death and burial his colleagues had moved on to Pernois, about seven miles away. They were informed of his death and burial the following day during a church parade service.

While in Beauval, George made two visits to the town's large and ornate cathedral. On the 22 October 1915 he visited along with John Hunter. On this occasion something caught his eye because the very next day he returned with his camera and took a photograph (overleaf) inside the building, of a statue of Joan of Arc. Today the statue remains inside the cathedral though its location has changed. It has been moved from a position on the left of the entrance door to a prominent position in front of the congregation, to the

right of the pulpit, where it can be seen by all who enter the building. The original plinth remains where it was at the time of Hackney's visit and could be easily missed.

His taking of this photograph begs the question, why? Was it because the story of Joan of Arc was well known at home, that of a heroine who defended her homeland against invasion or was the reason slightly more subtle?

When we examine the tunic on the statue it can be seen that it is decorated with the traditional French heraldic fleur-de-lis symbols. They can also be seen on the flag she carries in the photograph and on the actual statue today. The fleur-de-lis may have had a significant meaning to George because it was the symbol embroidered on the badge worn by the battalion scouts.

At 8.30 am on the morning of the 26 October 1915 the battalion left Beauval and began the march to the front line for the first time. They marched initially to the village of Couin where they stayed under canvas for one night encamped in the grounds of the local chateau. Hackney photographed the tented accommodation as it was, with tents laid out among the tree lined avenues that radiated from the chateau across the grounds.

The following morning they continued the march through Souastre, where they collected blankets before moving on to Fonquevillers and the front line. George, aware of his changing surroundings photographed men from the battalion en route to Fonquevillers while they rested at the side of the road. In this photograph George identified Fred Gaffikin seated on the right of the photograph eating.

He also took a photograph of the church at Fonquevillers which, in contrast to the splendid building at Beauval, had been almost completely destroyed by shell-fire. His photograph shows the crucifix still attached to the church wall on the right of the building at an angle to his view.

The front line at Fonquevillers faced the German positions at Gommecourt, so the church was only about 100 yards from the front. During this initial spell in the line the Young Citizens were under the supervision of guides from the 5th and 7th Battalions of the Royal Warwickshire Regiment. George's first night under enemy fire was generally uneventful except for the activities of the ever-present rats. He recorded in his diary:

"On arrival at the reserve trench we were allowed to go to sleep but of course were fully dressed ready to turn out at a moment's notice. We have the pleasure of the company of plenty of rats, which frequently march over our faces etc: some of the fellows do not seem to mind this but personally I am not particularly fond of them so was occasionally woken by their movement but on the whole I had a fair night's sleep."

The YCVs held the line at Fonquevillers until the 2 November when they were relieved and proceeded via Couin back to their old billets at Beauval. They had suffered two casualties: a sergeant, wounded by a fragment of a rifle grenade and one man who was part of a wiring party and was injured by a piece of barbed wire which fragmented on being struck by a burst of machine-gun fire.

As time moved on the men drew closer to experiencing their first Christmas at the front. For half of the battalion

it would be their first Christmas away from home as the previous year, in December 1914, those men were allowed home from Finner. The syllabus of infantry training continued along with trench digging and wood cutting. The men moved through various billets spending most of November 1915 in Pernois before moving to the village of Ailly-Le-Haut-Clocher, just a couple of miles north of

The blue line indicates the British front line and the red lines detail
the German trench system.

the River Somme itself and then to nearby Ergines on the 11 December 1915.

The Christmas scene was set with the first fall of snow but this was quickly replaced with heavy rain. As the battalion continued with their training programme right through December 1915 Christmas was spent away from the front line in relative comfort billeted in the village of Pernois.

George and his colleagues made trips to nearby Ailly-Le-Haut-Clocher to purchase cards to send home while those fortunate enough to receive parcels from home pooled their delicacies to produce passable Christmas dinners.

When George's friend, Paul Pollock, received such a parcel on Wednesday the 21 December, a dinner was hastily arranged for the occupants of George's billet. He photographed the scene and recorded the details in his diary:

"Wed 21st
Rose, nothing the worse for the wetting and paraded with the Coy for Coy drill but from which I was dismissed to act as Orderly Sergeant to relieve

Sergt. Scott while he was away with the bathing party but I had no calls to attend to so had a quiet morning. The bathers returned at 2.30 pm and we had the afternoon off. Owing to Paul Pollock getting a large consignment of stuff from home we decided to have a bust up of a dinner so the nine of us managed to all get round a table of 30 inches diameter and have an eight-course dinner, a dinner which we all thoroughly enjoyed. The courses were as follows:

Turkey
Boar's Head
Plum Pudding
Pineapple
Raisons and almonds
Figs and dates
Chocolates
Tea and cake
It was certainly a surprise dinner to have under the circumstances in which we were placed."

In his photograph the small table can clearly be seen as can the lengths that the men went to in order to make the kitchen of the French Billet resemble, as much as possible, Christmas at home.

George named seven of the eight men photographed and of those seven, four have been identified. They are, at far left, John Ewing; second from left at back, John Yarr; beside him at the back is John Currie and looking hauntingly at the camera, fourth from right is Paul Pollock. Also in the photograph is WJ 'Gus' Reid, John Pollock and Fred Moore.

The 14th Battalion of the Royal Irish Rifles ended 1915 with a number of impromptu concerts and parties around their billets, encouraged by their officers who had authorised the issue of rum and cognac to the men late on New Year's Eve. They were all apprehensive about what the New Year had in store but were buoyed with the youthful enthusiasm and energy that had formed the Young Citizen Volunteers in the first place. They could not have known how severe would be the trials that lay ahead of them as they celebrated the cold dawn of 1916.

THE NEW YEAR AND BERNEUIL

For George 1916 began with the rudest of awakenings by having the Company Sergeant Major inform him that he had slept in and was twenty minutes late for parade. He quickly discovered that the remainder of 'B' Company had also slept in and the morning parade on the 1 January 1916 had been cancelled. After breakfast the battalion was formed up and addressed by Colonel Chichester who had just retaken command and had returned from Belfast with New Year's greetings from the Lord Mayor. George's spirits were lifted by the address:

> "Somehow it felt like being nearer home seeing the familiar face and hearing the familiar voice of our original CO once more and whom we were glad to get back again."

The syllabus of infantry training continued along with the working parties detailed to repair billets and roads and dig trenches. George continued to document the experiences with his camera. At some time between the 15–23 January he took a number of photographs in and around Berneuil. The first is a view of Berneuil taken in January 1916. The pond on the left of the photograph has since been filled in.

In the second a fatigue party is photographed at Berneuil. George Cathcart and Sam Stansfield are named as part of the group but cannot be specifically identified.

The battalion spent most of January at Berneuil carrying on with training and supplying men to form various working and fatigue parties carrying out basic but essential jobs that included sweeping the village roads and maintaining and improving billets. On a number of occasions George accompanied the horse drawn limbers to nearby Montrelet where supplies of coal and wood were collected and brought back to Berneuil.

He photographed one of these parties showing Sergeant George William Clarke, from 431 Lisburn Road in Belfast seated at the rear of the limber. The inclusion of Sergeant Clarke helps with the dating of the photograph as we know from battalion records that he was sent to Le Havre for dental treatment on the 23 February 1916 and remained there until the 31 March, by which time the battalion had moved on to the Hamel sector, close to Thiepval. George Clarke was later wounded during action on the 1 July 1916 and eventually evacuated to hospital on the 13 July. He was finally discharged from military service on the 14 September 1918, four years exactly from the date he enlisted at the Old Townhall in Belfast in 1914.

On the 23 January 1916 Reverend John Crozier, Archbishop of Armagh and Primate of All Ireland, visited the 14th battalion at Berneuil. He conducted an open air drumhead service in the courtyard of one of the billets along with the Reverend Canon Richard King of Limavady, Colonel Chichester, who had just returned as the battalion commanding officer, and Adjutant Captain Mulholland.

Canon King held a number of church parades with the battalion and, at the time that the photograph below was taken he had recently lost his eldest son, 2nd Lieutenant Robert Andrew Ferguson King, who was mortally wounded during the 2nd Battle of Ypres on the 10 May 1915 while serving with the 2nd Battalion The Royal Dublin Fusiliers. Robert was 19 years old when he died of his wounds nearly two weeks later on the 23 May 1915 at the military hospital in Boulogne.

George photographed the service from an elevated vantage point. This photograph gives us one of the first indications of his standing as 'unofficial' battalion photographer. He did not take the photograph from amongst the ranks of the party assembled and he was in the sight and presence of the commanding officer.

While at Berneuil the men were issued with their goatskin coats as a protection against the cold. The issue and wearing of the coats caused some amusement among the men and provided excellent photographic subject matter for George. He took two group photographs of members of 'B' Company which he entitled "The Hairy Men".

Another shot taken at the same time and with the same backdrop shows John Currie and John Boyd playing 'wheelbarrow'. This shot is particularly interesting as it shows a spoon falling from John Currie's puttee. The men often carried what they called a 'racing spoon' in this manner so that it would always be at hand whenever the opportunity of a meal arose. Both John Boyd and John Currie survived the war. John Boyd, from 8 Rotterdam Street in Belfast was wounded in 1916 during the 1 July attack and evacuated home. John Currie, from 10 Chadolly Street in Belfast was injured and rejoined the battalion only to be wounded on two more occasions between late 1916 and mid 1917.

George, obviously aware of the comic value of such a photograph had someone operate his camera in order to take a photograph (opposite) of himself (right) along with his best friend John Ewing, both wearing their 'hairy' coats.

He also took time to record scenes of everyday life that interested him as with this photograph of the local windmill at Berneuil which has now disappeared completely.

He also photographed a local farmer working his land with a horse drawn plough. These scenes, without doubt, reminded him of Ireland and would be in stark contrast to what he was about to experience as the Young Citizens moved closer to the front.

George's final photograph in the series taken in Berneuil shows a group of 'B' Company soldiers having a joke with two French girls. George named this scene differently in two sets of his archive. In his France album it is titled "Hawkers at a French Village". This could be a reference to the practice of collecting tunic buttons, cap badges and other souvenirs by the local villagers. In another album the same photograph is entitled "Caught On" which may have been a jibe by George at one of the men in the photograph for becoming overly familiar with the locals.

George named four of the men in this scene, two of whom can be identified. The man at the centre of the main group looking at the camera, William James Hughes came from 217 Ainsworth Avenue in Belfast. He was the son of a Royal Irish Constabulary sergeant and had a brother, Robert who at that time was in officer training and would eventually serve as a captain in the Royal Inniskilling Fusiliers. William was wounded during the 1 July attack and hospitalised. He rejoined the 14th (YCV) Battalion almost a year later on the 18 June 1917 when it was involved in consolidating ground taken during the successful 7 June attack at Whytschate. Just two days later, while clearing captured enemy positions in the Oostaverne sector of the Belgian front, William was once again wounded by shell-fire that killed five other members of the battalion. Both he and his brother Robert eventually survived the war.

To the right of Hughes, carrying a pack and looking over his shoulder towards the camera is Rifleman Harry Moorehead. Harry lived at Shane's Lodge at the entrance to Shane's Castle in Randalstown. He took ill on the 25 May 1916 and was evacuated from the front. He was later discharged from the army on the 12 August 1916 suffering from valvular disorder of the heart (VDH).

The other men named by Hackney as being in this photograph were Fred Gaffikin and William Condell.

VARENNES AND ACHEUX

On the 8 February 1916 the battalion moved once again. Reveille at 5.30 am was followed by a parade in full kit at 9.00 am whereupon the men set off on a march to their next destination and new billets. In his diary George did not disclose the destination but we know from battalion records that they marched east to Puchvillers where they stayed for one night before moving again to Varennes.

From their billets in Varennes the battalion was marched daily into nearby Acheux where working parties were formed under the direction of Royal Engineers and their 16th Battalion Royal Irish Rifles pioneer colleagues. Their job was to help construct a new broad gauge railway and terminus through which the front line would be supplied with food, ammunition and equipment for the proposed 'big push'. At Acheux the men of the battalion would have considered themselves to be part of the bigger machine. They were for the meantime the battalion in reserve for the 36th (Ulster) Division and remained in the general area, either side of the River Ancre for the next number of months holding the line in rotation with the other Ulster battalions until the time was deemed right to make the attack. Acheux became a hub of military activity.

On Thursday the 10 February 1916, George described the action in the air as he marched to Acheux:

"Thurs 10th
Reveille 5.30 and after breakfast at 6.15 we paraded in drill order at 6.45 when we went away to help

with the construction of a railway, our part being digging. It was a glorious day and we saw plenty of aeroplanes, some of them hostile ones and they got quite a warm reception by our anti-aircraft guns. We got quite close to a big observation balloon and saw it rising; it was very interesting. We had dinner at our work and returned to our billets at 4.00…"

For the next few days George continued to work on the railway at Acheux. He took two photographs during his time there. The first shows a party of six men unloading logs from railway cars. George names five of the six men as John Yarr, WJ Hughes, Edgar Johnston, Austin McCleery, and Paul Pollock. Two of these men can be identified in the photograph, John Yarr, standing at far left and John Ewing, third from left.

The second photograph taken in this area shows Paul Pollock, John Ewing and John Yarr sitting in one of the railway trucks eating a meal from tinned food and from mess tins. Other mess tins can be seen at the right of the frame on the floor of the truck.

Paul Pollock was a good friend of George Hackney and was a member of St Enoch's Presbyterian Church in Belfast which was where George worshipped before the war and continued to attend for many years after the war. Paul's father, Reverend Alexander Pollock was the minister of St Enoch's at that time. He had visited the battalion while they were based at Liphook and had conducted a number of church services for the men before they left for France.

Paul Pollock was officially listed as "missing in action on or after the 1 July 1916". He was killed during the great battle and his body, like so many others, was never found. He was remembered on a stone plaque mounted in St Enoch's church but for reasons unknown his name was not recorded with the Commonwealth War Graves Commission until 2013 when it was eventually added to the Addenda Panel of the Thiepval Memorial To The Missing. Paul was 21 years old at the time of his death.

At the time he enlisted on the 28 May 1915 John Yarr lived at 38 Selby Street in Belfast with his wife May and five month old daughter, Sarah. On the 1 July 1916 he was injured during the attack at Thiepval by a gunshot wound to the right foot. He was evacuated home and after a long period of recovery was deemed fit enough to be transferred into the Labour Corps on the 28 July 1918. He was however re-examined on transfer resulting in him being medically discharged "surplus to military requirements" on 17 September 1918. In May of that year his wife gave birth to a son whom they had named William. For the new Yarr family the war was over and their lives could continue together.

BOMBING SCHOOL

On Monday the 14 February 1916 George paraded as usual and began his work at the railway. At lunch time he was told to report to the Brigade bombing school along with three others from 'B' Company for a course of instruction in bombing. In his diary George again omitted to include the location of the bombing school, leaving a blank space in the diary most probably as a precaution in the event that if he were captured this information would not fall into enemy hands. He left us a small clue in the photograph album when he described the bombing instruction photograph as simply "practice trenches". The 36th Ulster Division constructed replica German trenches close to the small hamlet of Clairfaye, west of Forceville and certainly within the marching distances George described. Here the battalions in the division took time out from the front line duties to practice attack techniques across a full scale 'model' landscape.

In true documentary photography fashion George continually made the effort to photograph what was new to him. It is for this reason that his photography stands out from other collections of the era. Although the subject matter may not be particularly interesting to us now he felt that new experiences were important enough for him to record and to use precious photographic material to preserve. It is interesting that although he took the precaution of censoring his own diary he continued to photograph the areas in which he found himself.

During his time at the bombing school for instance, he found himself billeted in new camouflaged pre-fabricated huts which were positioned close to the grenade throwing area. The school of instruction was also carried out in these huts; this kept the training billeting arrangements separate from the battalion billets and less of a drain on local resources. George photographed the huts with their disruptive pattern canvas camouflage.

Initially the training coincided with a storm with heavy rain turning to snow but George continued to photograph the various aspects of the training. By this time the new No 5 Mills grenade had been issued and was in use, replacing the No 1 stick-like percussion grenade that had been used previously. There can be little doubt that George took the training seriously. Just a week earlier on the 7 February, Sergeant William Calvert of 'A' Company had been killed accidentally while instructing a grenade class.

The new Mills grenades detonated after four seconds once the fuse was primed by releasing a spring loaded 'fly-off' lever. This lever was held in place by a pin which the soldier would extract using a ring pull when the weapon was being readied for use. The soldiers had to understand the mechanisms involved and know how to handle the weapon safely. It was described as a 'defensive' weapon which meant that it had to be used from a position of cover as it was not possible to out-run the shrapnel 'kill zone' within the four seconds available on the fuse. If a grenade was primed and dropped within the confines of a trench it was highly likely that death or injury would result unless those present were able to take cover around a traverse in the trench system. In two of George's photographs we can see bombing training actually taking place.

He has taken this photograph from a position close to the corner of the traverse in the trench system, the immediate foreground to the right of frame is blurred. We can see a warning flag marking the live training area. The man closest to the camera is a lance corporal in the Inniskilling Fusiliers who is standing in the bomb priming bay waiting to move up to the throwing area. In the distance a man is already in the throwing area behind another trench traverse. He has the grenade in one hand and with the other hand he is finding the ring pull before bringing the grenade up to chest level, pulling the pin while holding the fly-off lever in position and then throwing the grenade towards the target trench.

The next photograph shows a grenade exploding in the target trench. The man throwing the grenade would have had to indicate that it had actually landed in the target trench for Hackney to safely raise his head above the trench parapet to take the photograph of the explosion. If the grenade had landed on the level ground he would have risked injury from shrapnel flying horizontally in all directions.

George and his fellow students were able to relax and play football during down time between training sessions. He also photographed the snowy landscape at the training area.

OCEAN VILLAS

On the 20 February 1916 100 men of 'B' Company were detailed for duty under instruction in the trenches at Auchonvillers. Auchonvillers, or Ocean Villas as it was known to the troops, was an abandoned village on the front line facing the German positions at Beaumont Hamel between trench positions known as the Hawthorn Redoubt and The Redan. The period of instruction lasted only four days until 'B' Company rejoined the battalion and their railway work at Acheux. 'B' Company then returned to Auchonvillers with the rest of the YCV battalion for their first real period of holding the front line trenches as a complete fighting unit.

On the 24 February 1916 the battalion moved to billets in the village of Beaussart where they remained for three nights before being ordered to relieve the 10th Battalion of the Royal Irish Rifles in the centre sector of the Auchonvillers front. The Young Citizens made their way through the nearby village of Mailly-Maillet at dusk, passing batteries of artillery concealed beneath trees at the edge of the village. They entered the trenches beyond Auchonvillers as darkness fell after making their way across the gardens at the rear of the ruined houses of the deserted village as the main street was under direct observation from the enemy.

On returning to the trenches there had been a marked thaw in the freezing and snowy weather conditions that they had experienced up to then. As a result the men found the trenches filled with water from the melting snow. The situation was exacerbated by heavy rain. In some areas the water filled the trench up to knee height. Waterproof gum-boots, similar to modern-day fishing waders were provided as trench stores and handed over by the preceding unit. The condition of the gum-boots left a lot to be desired with men having to contend with holed, leaking boots. Some members of the battalion simply had to make do without any waterproof boots while others got by wearing two odd feet. By the time the battalion were relieved, on the night of the 3 March a number of men had reported sick suffering from trench foot.

'C' Company signaller Walter McCormack recorded the experience in his diary:

"We left for trenches at Auchonvillers, near Mailly-Maillet. This was a fairly quiet spot, and the only thing that annoyed us was the state of the trenches. The previous weeks rain left them in a frightful state. And when we took them over from the 10th Batt. we were up to the waist in rain and mud. It was unsafe to walk down trenches at night unless one could swim. And as soon as it got dark both officers and men preferred walking along the parapet. When our chaps took over not one of them had gum boots on, so they had to plough through the water, and as some of the sump-boards were floating about consequently some of the chaps got a bad wetting. They had to go

From left to right are Joe Johnston of 30 Coolbeg Street, Belfast who was wounded on the 1 July 1916; WJ Hughes, of 217 Ainsworth Avenue, Belfast; William Ruddy of 11 Balfour Street in Belfast and Victor Haslett, of 20 Elaine Street, Belfast.

William Ruddy was also injured on the 1 July 1916 and evacuated to base hospital five days later. On recovery he was admitted to cadet school where he was awarded a commission on the 31 July 1917 as a second lieutenant in the 4th Battalion of the Northumberland Fusiliers. Even as an officer he could not escape the wet and mud, and conditions such as he experienced in Auchonvillers would ultimately become a major factor in his death.

on guard with their wet clothing and it was here we had 6 cases of trench feet. But this state of affairs did not last long, and before we left that part of the line we had the trenches as dry as Royal Avenue. We left here, having no casualties."

George recorded the conditions with his camera. Initially he photographed the ruined village itself. In his first photograph (page 55) we are shown a scene of complete devastation. Between the ruined houses, destroyed by shell-fire, we can see the rotting carcasses of dead animals. Beyond, and at the centre of the frame George photographed his friend John Currie, surveying the scene.

In his second photograph above we again see a village destroyed, void of all inhabitants. The church, with ruined tower just visible in the distance did not escape damage.

George photographed a group of his colleagues from 'B' Company in the trenches at Auchonvillers. In the photograph we can see that the men are wearing their gum-boots and appear to be showing a cheerful face for the camera.

On the morning of the 26 October 1917 the 4th Northumberland Fusiliers, as part of 149th Brigade, mounted an attack on German bunkers and pillboxes in the area of the Turenne Crossroads at Passchendaele. Heavy rain combined with shell-fire had turned the battlefield into a quagmire. The plan of attack for the Tyneside men was to advance towards the enemy positions behind a series of artillery barrage 'lifts' and to take the enemy strongpoints before they could be re-occupied by the Germans coming up from their deep dugouts once the artillery ceased. The attacking battalions found themselves quickly bogged down in the now infamous mud of No-Man's-Land, unable to keep up with the artillery barrage and with sparse cover.

As the barrage passed their positions the Germans simply re-occupied their trenches and began to pick off the attacking troops with machine-gun and sniper fire as they floundered, exposed in the mud in front of them. The 4th Northumberland Fusiliers lost nine officers and 128 men before the end of the day, among them William Ruddy whose body was never recovered from the Passchendaele mud. His name was added to the 34,990 others on the Tyne Cot Memorial to the Missing.

The last photograph (below) shows an area known as 'The White City' at Auchonvillers with German trenches just visible as white lines in the distance.

FROM FORCEVILLE TO HAMEL

George's next move took him to the village of Forceville, approximately five miles west of the River Ancre. The specialist troops in the battalion, scouts, snipers, Lewis gunners and signallers were always relieved early by their counterparts in incoming battalions in order to allow time to take over specialist positions and equipment. The advantage of an early relief meant that these men had first pick of the billets at a new location.

We can see a group of such specialists in the next two photographs taken by George. They show a group of lance corporals, the same rank as George at that time, being led by a Sergeant on the road to Forceville and were most likely taken on the 3 March 1916 following the relief of the YCV battalion from the trenches at Auchonvillers.

In the first photograph (left) we see, from left to right, Lance Corporals James Fitzsimmons, Jim Cull, Bertie Kenny, William King and Sergeant John Kenning, in charge of the group. On close examination it can be seen that a few pieces of notable equipment are being carried. Jim Cull for instance is carrying a binoculars case slung across his left shoulder. Binoculars were only issued to 'other ranks' when they were involved in scouting or sniping duties. In the centre of the photograph Bertie Kenny is carrying a wooden box, the contents are obviously unknown but it may contain signalling equipment.

Most interesting is the item being carried by William King, second from right. What is believed to be a German M1916 'Stalhelm' helmet can be seen attached to his webbing. The appearance of this helmet in the photograph is significant as helmets of this new design were only known to have been issued to German troops operating in the Verdun sector and the YCV battalion, up to this time had experienced no contact with the enemy by way of trench raids or the taking of enemy positions or prisoners which might otherwise have explained its presence as a trophy.

In the second photograph above we see the same group of men continuing to make their way across the snowy landscape to Forceville.

Sergeant John Kenning, from 39 Sandhurst Drive in Belfast, was promoted to Company Quartermaster Sergeant the following month in April 1916. He survived the war.

Lance Corporal Hubert Stanley (Bertie) Kenny was a Lewis gunner. He lived at 112 Rugby Avenue in Belfast. He was eventually promoted to Sergeant in the 14th Battalion before being recommended for commission, following which he was appointed Second Lieutenant in the Royal Irish Regiment on the 26 March 1918. He was later wounded but survived the war.

Lance Corporal James Cull had just rejoined the battalion from Base Hospital on the 27 February, six days before this photograph was believed to have been taken. Ten days after the photograph was taken he was injured by shrapnel at Hamel during a bombardment. He rejoined his company again on the 24 July 1917 and three weeks later on the 16 August 1917 he was reported 'missing in action' following the battalion's engagement in the Battle of Langemark. His body was never recovered. He is remembered on the Tyne Cot Memorial to the Missing in Belgium.

Lance Corporal William King was a journalist before the war. On enlisting he named his sister as his next of kin with her address as Ardville, Dunmurry. William was reported as 'missing in action' following the battle at Thiepval on the 1 July 1916. He is remembered on the Thiepval Memorial to the Missing. He was 33 years old.

James Fitzsimmons (left) was one of three brothers in the YCV battalion. He served in the ranks along with his younger brother John, or 'Jack' as he was known. James was a first class bomber and was awarded the Military Medal for gallantry in the field during the 1 July battle, the same day his brother Jack was killed. Jack Fitzsimmons lies at rest in Connaught Cemetery at Thiepval.

Their elder brother, Ernest was teaching at the time war broke out. He joined the Queen's University Belfast Officer Training Corps and was commissioned into the same battalion as his two brothers. Ernest served as battalion bombing and specialist training instructor before becoming brigade intelligence officer. He distinguished himself on the 7 June 1917 during the battle of Whytschate in Belgium where he was in command of signals and communications on the battlefield. Following this he was promoted and moved to general staff. He survived the war and remained in France until October 1921 serving as a Major in the Department of Graves Registration and Enquiry, a forerunner of the Commonwealth War Graves Commission. In this role he was awarded the MBE for his part in planning the operation to recover the body of The Unknown Warrior and supervising the operation on the French side of the channel. On eventually leaving France from this position he was one of the last four remaining original British Expeditionary Force (BEF) soldiers to leave the war area. In later life he settled in Dublin where he became a Barrister at Law.

After spending three nights at Forceville George and the Young Citizens moved closer to the front again to the village of Mesnil. Here they billeted in the cellars of the ruined houses in the village and carried out regular reliefs on the front line positions at Hamel.

George continued to document his experiences as in his photograph opposite of the sun setting beyond the village and the fatigue party carrying bath water for the men through the ruined village. In the latter, for the first time in George's photographs, we can see the men of the battalion wearing their newly issued helmets.

In this photograph George names Sam Stansfield as being part of the group. Unfortunately at this time he cannot be identified.

Taking their turn in and out of the front line, the battalion remained in the Mesnil and Hamel areas for the greater part of a month. In this sector they began to suffer their first real casualties to artillery shelling behind the lines around their billets and trench mortar bombardments on their front lines.

One of the main communication trenches between Mesnil and Hamel was known as Jacob's Ladder. It ran for a considerable distance downhill starting from a point just north of Mesnil and ending at the edge of Hamel village on the Ancre Valley floor as seen on the map opposite.

Jacob's Ladder was for most of its length, in full view of the German positions across the valley and was regularly swept by enemy machine-gun fire. A party of men clean up Jacob's Ladder in the photograph below.

The blue lines (including minor red lines linking them) indicate the
British trenches and the red lines (top and bottom right) show the
German trenches.

HAMEL

For most of April 1916 the YCV battalion rotated between six day spells in the front line followed by six days out of the line at Mesnil. They were gradually being exposed to increasingly dangerous sectors as they added experience gained in the trenches to their syllabus of training. George continued to photograph the world around him, a world that had become gradually more and more alien and removed from his life in Belfast. He photographed landscapes from positions around the destroyed village of Hamel along with scenes of the ruined village itself.

These particular photographs can hint at the type of soldier that George Hackney was. They show in detail the enemy positions and would be of obvious intelligence value to his senior officers as they planned for 'the big push'.

They have been taken from points right on the front lines. In taking them George would have exposed himself to a considerable level of risk being under constant threat of enemy sniper fire. One explanation offered is that George may have been a scout or even a sniper himself and took these photographs from observation points for both his own and battalion intelligence use. There are no battalion official records naming him as a sniper, but then again there are no records naming any individual in the battalion as a sniper. Scouts are named in battalion records but the categorising of the scouts is not consistent throughout the records with some named and photographed members of the scout section, or 'Permanent Patrol' as it was known, not actually having been listed in the battalion roll as scouts and vice-versa.

George left us no clue as to the exact nature of his duties as his own diary for this period of the war has unfortunately been lost. The missing volume covered the period from the 18 February 1916 to the 21 July 1917, when the YCV battalion was engaged in combat during the build up and the attack on the 1 July 1916.

The first photograph opposite, of obvious intelligence use, shows a view of what was to be the battlefield at Thiepval from a trench position at the edge of Hamel village. It was most likely taken from a trench known as Joffre Avenue that ran between two communication trenches known as Connantray Avenue and Hedgerow Avenue. The chalk spoil parados of the British trenches can be seen on the left foreground as they crest the brow of the hill towards the River Ancre. In the distance we can quite clearly see Thiepval Wood at the far right of the frame with the Sunken Road bending to the left towards the top of Thiepval Ridge. Moving left we then see the white chalk lines of the German trenches running parallel to the Sunken Road up to the top of the ridge to the point where the Ulster Tower stands today.

The front across which the Ulster Division advanced on the 1 July was greater than the area covered by this photograph by some considerable distance beyond the left of the frame. It must be remembered that the German machine-gunners on the 1 July would have had a similar field of view, and indeed field of fire, from positions just forward of where George took this photograph. One can begin to understand how vulnerable the men were during the attack from the incessant enfilading fire brought down upon them from this side of the valley as they pushed forward their advance.

Below left George has taken a photograph from a position close to the previous shot but further into the village of Hamel itself. The view appears to be from a position close to where the village church stands today on the Rue D'Eglise. We can see the completely destroyed houses and possibly the entrance to a cellar dugout at the centre of the frame. Again the German positions are ever-present, dominating the skyline in the background.

The scene today shows modern houses rebuilt in almost the same positions as those of a century ago.

Opposite we see the men improving or repairing one of the dugouts at Mound Keep. John Ewing is at the right of the photograph with Charlie Blake looking at the camera.

Rifleman Charles Blake joined the YCV battalion in France as part of the first reinforcement on the 16 December 1915. He had lived at 245 Crumlin Road, Belfast with his widowed mother, Margaret, and was one of the 44 members of the battalion killed in action during the successful attack at Whytschaete in Belgium on the 7 June 1917. He is buried at Spanbroekmolen Cemetery, a cemetery almost exclusively occupied by the graves of YCV soldiers. Spanbroekmolen Cemetery is situated close to the site of the detonation of a massive mine, one of a series detonated beneath the German positions which marked the start of the attack.

George continued to record the devastation he observed around him, above a destroyed barn beneath a fall of snow close to the River Ancre.

Mound Keep

After each relief from their tour of duty in the trenches at Hamel the YCV battalion, on leaving the line and moving to their billets in Mesnil, was required to supply one platoon of men to occupy the railway and road checkpoint at Mound Keep for a period of 24 hours at a time. Mound Keep consisted of a number of dugouts and trenches built at the edge of the Ancre Swamp at a point where the Mill Road crossed the railway that ran parallel to the River Ancre. The dugouts were, by all accounts, relatively comfortable and the spell of duty there was one that was not disliked by the men.

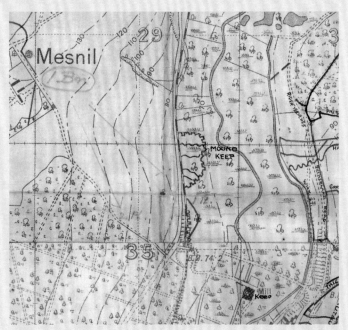

With permission of the Deputy Keeper of the Records, Public Record Office of Northern Ireland, D3835/E/11/7

Pictured above, a section of 'B' Company relaxing in the spring sunshine outside a dugout built into the railway embankment at Mound Keep. Those that can be identified to date are: extreme left, John Currie; third from left, John Yarr; fourth from right (reading), WJ (Gus) Reid; third from right, Paul Pollock; and second from right John Ewing.

Also named as being in the photograph but not specifically identified are Fred Moore and John Pollock. A further soldier appears but is not named. This group contains the same personalities as the Christmas photograph taken 21 December 1915 (page 37).

Sentry Post at Hamel

This remarkable photograph adds weight to the suggestion that George was part of a scout/sniper section. The photograph was annotated by George as: "Sentry Post At Hamel". It shows a group of four men at the corner of a trench 'traverse' outside a heavily reinforced dugout or perhaps the entrance tunnel to a 'sap' or small trench allowing access to No-Man's-Land from the main front line trench. We can say that this trench is in the front line as it has been built with a 'fire-step', a step on which the occupants stood to fire over the parapet of the trench at the enemy. In previous photographs, such as those taken at Auchonvillers, the trenches did not have fire-steps, as they were communication trenches, used as protected access routes to and from the front line.

In this photograph the rifle at the left of the frame gives us perhaps the strongest indication of the role of its owner. The butt of the rifle has been modified by having a cloth pad or most likely a field dressing wrapped around it. This

modification helped the user re-align his eye to either a telescopic or Galilean optical sight.

Sniping in the British army was in its infancy at the time this photograph was taken. There was no standard issue sight available to snipers with officers purchasing locally available items from sporting suppliers at home for use by their troops. One stipulation which was enforced was that whatever design of sight was fitted it could not obscure or cover the breech area so that the rifle remained capable of being loaded by using a five round clip or charger. This meant that any optics fitted to the Short Magazine Lee Enfield rifle (SMLE) had to be mounted along the side of the rifle barrel and not on top. The shooter had to then devise a way of resting his cheek away and to the left of the butt of the rifle to enable comfortable alignment of his right eye with the modified sight. In this photograph we can see just such a cheek modification in use at the front line. Unfortunately we cannot see the left side of the rifle to determine what type of sight, if any, is attached.

This particular type of rifle is interesting in itself. It is an older model of SMLE than those which had been issued to the men at Seaford before leaving for France. This rifle is fitted with a magazine cut-off plate which, when in use, cuts off the feed of rounds from the magazine with the result that the rifle has to be loaded by feeding individual rounds into the breech by hand. This method of operation would have been preferable to a sniper who, needing

always to be careful with his rounds, would not have risked damaging the head of the bullet by the action of having it rammed into the breech from the magazine. The ordinary infantryman, however, needed to load his ten rounds from the magazine as he was usually required to fire them off rapidly in a combat situation.

The rifle in the photograph also appears to have been fitted with a leather sling, as opposed to the standard issue webbing sling. The slightly more elastic properties of the leather was preferred by snipers who used the sling not just as a carrying aid but as a support when firing, wrapping it around the forearm to support the rifle. It is unclear which of the men in the photograph the rifle belongs to.

The man standing second from left is carrying a case for a set of binoculars; again binoculars were not an item that was issued to the ordinary infantryman and may indicate his specific role as being a scout, sniper or observer for a sniper.

The man on the left is Frederick Gaffikin who lived at 11 Cooke Street in Belfast at the time of his enlistment in September 1914. Fred took ill on the 19 May 1916 and was sent to base hospital. He returned on the 5 July and remained with the battalion as it moved into Belgium. He again reported ill on the 18 May 1917 and as a result was eventually discharged from military service on the 30 March 1918 suffering from the kidney disorder, nephritis.

As Fred Gaffikin was convalescing from his second bout of illness his elder brother, William Bertram Gaffikin enlisted to join the colours on the 17 September 1917. William had emigrated to Canada some years previously to follow his trade as an electrician. He lived in Toronto where he married his wife, Elsie on the 17 August 1914, just thirteen days after war was declared by Britain on Germany. He volunteered with the Princess Patricia's Canadian Light Infantry and quickly found himself in France. He was killed in action on the 28 September 1918 at Tilloy during the Canadian assault at the Canal Du Nord. An official report on his death states: "He was instantly killed by a sniper's bullet near the wood in front of Tilloy".

After the war Fred Gaffikin decided to emigrate to Canada where he also settled in Toronto and set up a florist business. In January 1924 he married Alice Morrow (left). They may have had many things in common, one of the greatest being that both had lost brothers in the war but Alice and Frederick had a further common bond – Alice's brother, Robert had served alongside Fred in the 14th Royal Irish Rifles (YCV).

Robert Morrow had been a signaller in 'C' Company. He was wounded during the 1 July attack and rejoined the battalion on the 11 August 1917 only to be killed in action five days later during the battle of Langemark.

Second from left in the trench photograph (page 69) is George Smyth Moore, a grocer's assistant from 11 Shaftesbury Square, Belfast. George Moore was in the line with the 14th Royal Irish Rifles, the YCV battalion, for the entire period that the battalion was in existence.

He was gassed on the 6 September 1918 while serving with an entrenching battalion following the disbandment of the Young Citizen Volunteers. He was evacuated to a base hospital and following a full year of convalescence, on the 11 September 1919 he was discharged from the army with "A1 health". George Moore crossed paths with the author's great-grandfather on the 19 December 1915. His conduct sheet states that he was "Absent from tattoo till 11.55 pm". For this offence he was reported by Sergeants Wallace Paton and Jimmy Scott and after a disciplinary hearing was fined five days wages. Nevertheless, after serving for almost exactly five years from his date of enlistment his discharge papers state that his conduct was "very good".

Third from left is James 'Jim' Herdman Johnston. The son of a commercial traveller, his family had lived at Church View in Holywood, County Down before moving to Seacliff Road in Bangor at the time of his enlistment in 1914. It is highly likely that the rifle, seen in the photograph on page 69 propped against the trench wall at the left of the frame, was his. He was highly regarded by his superiors and having been recommended for Cadet School, he was sent to England for officer training on the 7 October 1916. He was commissioned as a 2nd Lieutenant in the Royal Irish Rifles on the 28 March 1917 and survived the war as a Lieutenant.

On the extreme right is Sergeant George Brankin. George came originally from Fifth Street in Belfast before moving to 59 Frederick Street in Newtownards where he lived with his wife Mary at the time of enlistment. He was wounded on the 1 July at Thiepval. Following recuperation he rejoined the YCV battalion in the Dranoutre sector of the front line in Belgium as it made preparations for the next big attack. George Brankin led his platoon into battle at Whytschaete on the 7 June 1917. Overall the day went well for the Young Citizens; the attack commenced at 3.10 am and by 10.35 am the YCV had taken their objective at 'Jump Point' and raised the YCV flag at that position marking the completion of their allocated task. However Sergeant Brankin was mortally wounded in that attack and died of his wounds the following day at the casualty clearing station at Hazebrouck approximately 15 miles from the battlefield. He was laid to rest in Hazebrouck Communal Cemetery.

One additional photograph (right), which cannot be attributed directly to George Hackney, but which is included in the Ulster Museum Hackney lantern slide collection, also appears as an original print in the Royal Ulster Rifles Museum archive. It shows a Royal Irish Rifles sniper standing in low light, either about to go out on patrol at dusk, or just returning at dawn. He is photographed amongst ruined buildings close to the front line. This photograph is remarkable in that we can see the extent to which the sniper attempted to change his general shape and appearance by wearing a camouflaged 'gillie' suit.

More importantly we can see that close to the muzzle of the rifle the soldier has attached a 'Gallilean' optical sight which is mounted to the left of the original iron fore-sight. It is difficult to extract the detail in the image but the sight appears identical to one manufactured and supplied to the Royal Irish Rifles by Sharman D Neill Ltd of Belfast, called 'The Ulster' rifle sight. This particular type of sight, once mounted, would require the sniper to either aim using his left eye, difficult for those right handed and naturally 'right eyed' or to pad the left side of the butt of the rifle in exactly the manner which we see in George's photograph on page 69. An excellent example of 'The Ulster' sight can be seen on display today in the Royal Ulster Rifles Museum in Belfast. Photographs taken of British Army snipers during the Great War are particularly rare. A photograph showing this particular type of sight being used by a sniper in the field wearing a complete 'gillie' suit is unique. When we consider that this image turns up in collections in both the Ulster and RUR museums, and bearing in mind George Hackney's obvious access to the scout/sniper section in his battalion, it is fair to assume that it was either taken by him or is in fact a photograph of him.

Courtesy of the Royal Ulster Rifles Museum.

THIEPVAL WOOD, MAY 1916

On Easter Monday, the 24 April 1916, the men of 'B' Company accompanied by 'C' Company, marched into the Thiepval Wood area to familiarise themselves with their latest front line positions. The 11th Royal Inniskilling Fusiliers were in the line at that time. The following day officers from each company of the 14th Royal Irish Rifles (YCV) visited the wood to acquaint themselves with the topography of the area and specific locations of interest. On the 28 April the battalion War Diary records that orders were received to take over the trenches at Thiepval from the 11th Inniskillings. On the 30 April the remainder of The Young Citizen Volunteers completed the move into Thiepval Wood to hold the sector as a complete battalion. Before them, across No-Man's-Land and dominating the high ground, were the lines of German trenches and the system of fortifications and dugouts known as Fort Schwaben or the Schwaben Redoubt.

Initially the men found life in Thiepval Wood to be good. Spring had arrived and the wood was awakening from the winter in all its glory. They found the trenches in good order, with some areas even equipped with plumbed running water. Spirits were high. Signaller William McCormack wrote:

"It was fine. The trees were in full bloom and the birds were singing cheerily long before dawn. Cuckoos and larks were our chief delight here and of these we had plenty. In fact if it had not been for the occasional Ping! of a snipers bullet, Zip Zip Zip of a machine-gun and the roar of artillery one would have felt inclined to forget all about the war and fancy he was having an ideal holiday."

It wasn't long before the YCVs learnt to their cost that Thiepval Wood was not the idyllic country woodland that it first appeared. Casualties during the first week of May became an almost daily occurrence. The battalion was due to be relieved at Thiepval on the 6 May 1916 by the 9th Royal Inniskilling Fusiliers. On the night of the 5 May they were informed that a trench raid would be carried out by the 32nd Division just to the right of the 36th Division's sector. From the war diaries of the respective battalions an account of what happened can be patched together.

Throughout the afternoon of the 5 May the Germans shelled the British front lines between Thiepval village and the River Ancre, along the line of Thiepval Wood. The 16th Lancashire Fusiliers suffered two fatalities as a result of this shelling with a further seven men wounded. Meanwhile those men of the 15th Lancashire Fusiliers who had been selected to take part in the planned raid began to make their way from their reserve dugouts up to the front line. In total four officers, led by Captain MacLaren and Irishman, Captain Robert Smith from Naas in County Kildare, along with 50 men, took part. As darkness fell the leading groups of the raiding party began to arrive at the designated exit point on the British front line.

At 23.30 hrs battalion scouts, who had been deployed out in No-Man's-Land observing and listening for enemy activity returned to their lines reporting that all was clear. It was then decided that the raid would proceed. At this time a party of one Sergeant and three men moved out into No-Man's-Land bringing with them a Bangalore torpedo. This was an ammonal explosive device of tubular construction attached to interlocking sections of tubing which enabled it to be pushed beneath the enemy barbed wire and detonated remotely, the aim being to cut the enemy wire and create access to the German trenches. This party moved close to the enemy wire, laying brown and white coloured tape marking the correct route through their own maze of barbed wire for the remainder of the raiding party to follow. Ten minutes later the remainder of the raiding party moved out of their trenches in groups of four, separated by ten yard gaps and followed the tape across No-Man's-Land to a point approximately 130 yards away from the German lines, just short of the estimated half way point. There the raiders lay still to avoid detection and waited for what must have felt like an eternity. At this point if one man had 'showed out', broke the skyline or made any detectable noise it would have proved fatal for the entire party. Dangerously exposed with minimal cover in No-Man's-Land, each man depended on the effectiveness of his camouflage and concealment. Bayonets on rifles, carried only by a few men of the team, were blackened and helmets were covered in sacking or sand bag material. Most of the raiders carried bombs and revolvers, in addition to 'knobkerries' or trench clubs and fighting knives, were carried in preference to rifles as they would be easier to use in the confined space of the enemy trenches.

At the stroke of midnight a terrific artillery barrage was unleashed onto the German lines. The bombardment was directed across the planned point of entry into the German trenches on a front approximately 200 yards wide. This point of entry was located opposite the left flank of the 32nd Division sector, bordering on the sector held by the Young Citizens. It was planned that the raiding party would not carry out their raid directly opposite their own lines in order that their retreat would not be hindered by any retaliation.

Under the cover of the bombardment the advanced party along with the those carrying the Bangalore torpedo moved up to a position just sixty yards from the German line. The bombardment lasted 25 minutes, sweeping along the front line, across the point of entry and back again while arcing in a semi-circle to cover the flanks and rear of the area to be raided, thus protecting the raiding party from counter-attack. Fifteen rounds from a two inch trench mortar were then dropped as close to the actual proposed point of entry as possible in order to help the raid leader find his bearings. During the final minute of the bombardment the Sergeant and three men with the Bangalore torpedo moved forward and placed the ammonal tube into the German wire with the objective of blowing a hole through it.

Frustratingly, the torpedo failed to explode. Captain MacLaren immediately sent back for another Bangalore torpedo to be brought up to his position, acutely aware that the enemy, realising that the bombardment had stopped, could be re-emerging from their deep dugouts and in a position to repel their attack. Five nerve racking minutes later the second device arrived and was forced into the German wire alongside the first and primed. The second torpedo detonated successfully and also blew up the first torpedo which was lying beside it. The effect of the two devices exploding simultaneously cut a neat ten yard swathe through the concertina wire. The time was now 00.33hrs on the morning of the 6 May 1916.

Along the front line, at the very edge of the 36th (Ulster) Division sector, the Young Citizen Volunteers had been 'stood to arms' at their posts, manning the fire-step of the forward trench at Thiepval Wood. Meanwhile the Lancashire Fusiliers went about their deadly business in the German front lines with four 'snatch' teams quickly moving from dugout to dugout, man-handling prisoners out of their protection and bringing them out of the trench where other members of the raiding party covered their return to the British lines. Two prisoners were taken almost immediately and a further three followed within minutes. In total five prisoners were taken and a number of the dugouts were bombed.

A half-hearted attempt was made to counter-attack the raiding party but this was repulsed using grenades. Nevertheless despite their success the Lancashires had suffered casualties. The bodies of five of their party, killed during the raid, were carried back across No-Man's-Land to their own lines. As the raiders left the enemy lines the Germans began their retaliation, initially using trench mortars but following up with a deadly artillery barrage onto the sector of trenches directly opposite the point of entry made on their positions by the raiding party.

Almost immediately the battalion headquarters of the 14th Royal Irish Rifles was rocked by a large mortar explosion, night turned to day with the intensity of the retaliatory bombardment. Lieutenant Walker ordered his company to 'stand to' at their posts anticipating a counter raid. The men of 'D' Company turned out of their protective funk holes and dugouts and manned the fire-step of their front line encouraged by their Commander. Throughout the bombardment, Walker paced up and down behind his men shouting cheerful encouragement in anticipation of finally engaging his enemy, keeping his men ready at their posts. In the headquarters dugout, named 'Gordon Castle', the situation was beginning to look increasingly serious to Captain Harper. Communication by telephone with 'D' Company had been lost at an early stage of the bombardment, followed by loss of communication between the YCV battalion and the 16th Lancashire Fusiliers on their right. The wires for the field telephones had been severed by exploding shells. Any communication now had to be made by runners, risking death to carry information to and from the companies in the line. This activity was severely hampered by German machine-gun fire sweeping through the barrage along the British support and communication trenches.

At approximately 01.25 hrs a runner, Rifleman Milligan from Roden Street in Belfast, made it to Gordon Castle having come through a wall of shell-fire from 'D' Company's line and reported that they had suffered 10 casualties. The artillery fire had become so intense that the exploding shells began to bring down trees in the wood which crashed to the ground across the trenches, further hampering communications. Eventually, with the bombardment at its peak, a trench protecting a platoon of 'D' Company collapsed, burying alive the men in it.

At 02.30 hrs Lieutenant Walker regained communications with his headquarters after a telephone wire had been re-laid by a signaller. He reported "a number of his men had been buried by a trench coming in on them". The full extent of the carnage inflicted now became apparent. A squad of men led by Pioneer, Sergeant Tom Murphy, began frantically digging in an attempt to rescue their colleagues, exposing themselves to heavy machine-gun and shell-fire as they worked. The Lewis Gun teams, brought together by Lance Corporal Steele began laying down covering fire as those members of the battalion not engaged in holding the line began to excavate the collapsed trench in a frantic rescue operation. At around this time a shrapnel shell exploded directly above Lieutenant Walker decapitating him and also killing Rifleman Edward Adams who was beside him at the time.

Chaos reigned right along the sector. At Hammerhead Sap, a part of the front line trench system close to the now ruined Thiepval Chateau, a similar story was unfolding. The sap had been used to site one of the 109th Brigade Machine Gun Company's Vickers machine-guns. During the bombardment the gun and team were also buried alive along with seven or eight men of the 16th Lancashire Fusiliers. One of the gunners, Private Thomas Bottoms who was from Durham and who had previously served with the Royal Inniskilling Fusiliers, somehow managed to extricate himself from the debris and then, under heavy fire, used his own entrenching tool to dig out the remainder of the buried men, saving their lives. The gun itself was also recovered the next morning, still intact. Thomas was awarded the Military Medal for his actions that night. He was killed on the 1st July 1916. His name appears on the Thiepval Memorial to the Missing.

By 03.00 hrs on the morning of the 6 May the barrage died down and a period of relative quiet returned to Thiepval Wood. The men of the 14th Royal Irish Rifles 'stood to arms' as dawn broke and the roll was called. There were many who did not answer. Signaller McCormack described the scene:

"When dawn appeared our front line was completely levelled to the ground and it was practically impossible to move along the trenches as huge trees were lying across them. But when one looked across at the other side they were even worse than our own, as it was impossible to distinguish between their trenches and our shell holes."

During the bombardment the casualties were evacuated by stretcher bearers along the evacuation route out of Thiepval Wood where they were then transferred to hand carts and taken a distance of about a quarter of a mile to the dressing station at the village of Authuile. Here the dead were buried and the more seriously wounded were transferred by ambulance to the dressing station at Forceville, some six miles away on the far side of the River Ancre. There they were assessed and treated before being either returned to duty or moved on to a Casualty Clearing Station away from the front lines and from where they could eventually be evacuated further, to a hospital in England or closer to home in Ireland.

For the 15th Lancashire Fusiliers the raid on the night of the 5 May was deemed a success. Five German prisoners had been taken and twenty of the enemy were estimated to have been killed in their dugouts. For what was described as a "successful" raid the Lancashires had paid a high price. The Irishman leading the raid, Captain Robert John Smith was killed as was his 20 year old 2nd Lieutenant, John Ramsay Younger from Manchester along with Sergeant Brooks and Privates Wall and Leeming from Salford. Five others were wounded. In addition to the 15th Lancashires' casualties the 16th Lancashires on the front line lost one man with fourteen wounded. The 2nd Royal Inniskilling Fusiliers manning the sector to the right of the 16th Lancashires lost two men with another fourteen wounded.

The 14th Royal Irish Rifles (YCV) suffered dearly. In addition to the loss of Lieutenant Walker, the first of their officers to be killed in action, twelve men were killed and a total of twenty nine were wounded with two later dying of their wounds. In total, the casualties along the Thiepval sector on the morning of the 6 May 1916 numbered three officers and eighteen men killed with sixty-two wounded. That morning the men of the 14th Royal Irish Rifles along with the Lancashire Fusiliers cleared up the debris in their trenches and buried their dead at the cemetery at Authuile.

The Young Citizens were relieved in the line by the 9th Inniskilling Fusiliers and marched to their hut billets beside Martinsart. There they spent Sunday the 7 May cleaning equipment and catching up with much needed sleep. They left the Thiepval area the following day for new billets at Lealvillers.

George Hackney's series of photographs recording his time in Thiepval Wood during May 1916 reflect the written accounts and official documents which are available.

At this particular point in his photography we can sense a change in mood conveyed to us visually through the lens of his camera. In the photographs taken before May 1916 we see scenes of happy men, joking and larking about, making the most of the circumstances in which they found themselves. Photographs of young men in soldier's uniforms but they were not yet soldiers in the sense that they had yet to experience the full horrors of battle. We can sense a metamorphosis of subject matter as the adventure switched before George's eyes to the serious business of war. The series of photographs evolves through scenes of the men washing to portraits taken in the wood, to the damaged and broken trees and destruction ending with the grave of George Kirkwood leaving us with the stark image of a friendship lost.

This photograph below left, taken by George, is the last photograph we have of his friend Paul Pollock before he was killed and reported "missing in action" after the attack from these positions on the 1 July 1916, just six or

seven weeks from when the photo was taken. Paul is photographed standing along with Norman Donaldson who has stripped to his waist in order that his body and clothing can be checked for lice, a common parasitic pest that constantly plagued the men while in the trenches. Paul is assisting in this unpleasant task. The photograph was taken at a location named by the Ulster soldiers as "Antrimvillers" with an obvious hint to home. Antrimvillers had been located at the rear of Thiepval Wood in an area where the wood falls steeply down to the River Ancre. The approximate location of this photograph can be established today as the pathways, cut into the slope by the soldiers, still remain visible. This area, with its steep bank, was believed to be safe from direct fire from the German positions at Thiepval and also from German artillery fire on account of the leeward slope being difficult for the artillery to range onto without using an exceptionally steep trajectory. From George's photographs the area certainly appears to be one in which the men feel safe enough to carry out their daily personal tasks.

George also took a portrait of Lieutenant Thomas Hudson Mayes (right) outside his dugout 'Hazel Villas'. Thomas was an accountant in civilian life and returned to accountancy after surviving the war. He was also the subject of one of George's final photographs taken later in Belgium (see page 106).

A series of photographs show the landscape across the River Ancre viewed from "Antrimvillers". In the first below, men can be seen washing themselves and cleaning clothing and equipment.

The scene today has changed little. The woodland has thickened out and the laneway that follows the edge of the slow flowing river in a wide arc in the direction of Authuile can still be seen. This pathway, called Le Bordeau on modern maps, was named Speyside on trench maps of the area back in 1916. Today it makes for a pleasant walking route between the bottom of the infamous Sunken Road where it joins the Route de Saint Pierre Divion to where it runs south, eventually joining the Rue de Grandcourt just north of Authuille Village. A century ago this was a major route for supplies of stores and ammunition going in to the Thiepval Wood trench system and also the evacuation of casualties. A narrow gauge railway was built along part of its length. Walking the route today depressions in the ground, the remains of dugouts and gun pits, can still be seen in the steep bank that ascends from the riverbank.

When the photograph is viewed with the next two shots in the sequence (pages 80–81) it can be seen that the three shots were taken by George from almost the same spot on the slope at Antrimvillers, a few metres above the pathway. By joining these three shots we have a remarkable, almost 180 degree panoramic view of the scene along Speyside on an early evening in May 1916 which includes groups of men washing at the side of the river apparently unperturbed by shells exploding in the distance. It is clear that the men believed they were in a place of relative safety.

George's technique in photographing this scene by using multiple images gives us a far deeper insight into his creative and technical abilities. In the albums of prints that survive, the three images were never 'joined' to show the completed scene as printed photographs. Nevertheless I still cannot help but believe that he intentionally photographed the

scene in this way in order to record a wide panorama. This early attempt at joiner photography, a technique not seen again until the 1980s when it was pioneered by artist David Hockney, highlights a high level of skill, imagination and confidence in using his equipment to record a panoramic scene wider than the capabilities of his relatively simple camera.

In these photographs we can see the destruction caused by German shelling of the trenches at Thiepval Wood. These photographs were most likely taken on the morning of the 6 May 1916 just before George and the YCV battalion left the Thiepval area.

One photograph (above right) shows a trench with a fire-step confirming that it is the front line. Extensive damage can be seen beyond the sandbagged barricade. This coincides with the accounts of the 5/6 May bombardment which describe the right section of the line being the target of deadly artillery fire. It was in this area that a number of men of 'D' Company were buried alive when the front line trench collapsed during the bombardment. Those killed, Lieutenant Jerome Walker and nine of his men, are buried together at the little cemetery at Authuile overlooking the River Ancre.

The author's great-grandfather, Sergeant Jimmy Scott of 'B' Company, at some point that day paused to record their names in a pocket diary which he carried with him. He had previously recorded the names of the men he had lost from his own company along with the names of the cemeteries in which they were buried and the dates they were killed. He obviously decided to widen his criteria and record the names of these men also, even though they were not from 'B' Company; they were brothers together. An experienced soldier, he had perhaps learnt the importance of recording such details for families and loved ones back home. This was the last time he recorded such a list. The next occasion where he would have had cause to put pencil to paper would be the 1 July 1916. The book would simply not have been big enough and the task of recording the dead on that date, impossible for him.

The book containing the names was returned to his widow along with his personal effects after he was killed in action at Messines on the 22 January 1917. It remains with the Scott family today.

One man, mortally injured in the 6 May bombardment, died of his wounds three days later at the dressing station at Forceville, some six miles away from Thiepval Wood. He was Rifleman George Kirkwood (below left) who had lived at Alexandra Park Avenue in North Belfast. He was well known in the area being a top footballer with the local Brantwood FC and a member of the congregation of Castleton Presbyterian Church. He also played football for

the YCV 'B' Company football team and was a member of the 1915 Regimental Cup winning team. As a member of the 'B' Company Lewis Gun section he was a specialist soldier. In civilian life he was an engine fitter, a trade which undoubtedly helped him to quickly understand the working parts and mechanism of a machine-gun.

George Hackney took two photographs of George Kirkwood's grave. In the first photograph we can see the grave site at Forceville Cemetery. The grave stands out from the others nearby with its decorative fence and an edging of white chalk and flint stone, the like of which can be found just below the surface soil across the Somme area.

In the second photograph we can see that an additional grave cross has been placed in front of the standard military cross. The new cross has the YCV badge burnt into it along with the soldier's details, company and date

of death, instead of these being affixed on the standard stamped tin strip. This is the first time that we see this design of cross and later photographs show that they were used on the graves of all YCV fallen. The Young Citizen Volunteers stood apart from the other Royal Irish Rifles battalions not only with differences in cap badge and shoulder insignia but also in the unique way that they marked the graves of their fallen comrades, a hark back to their formation in 1912 and the principles that set them apart from the Ulster Volunteer Force regiments that also formed at that time.

Following their move out of the front line at Thiepval the YCV Battalion rested at Martinsart Wood on the opposite side of the River Ancre. They paraded for a church service and rested before moving to Lealvillers, some eight miles or so from the front line. Here they remained for over a month, marching to the nearby corps training area at Baizieux to practice attacking dummy German positions between periods of work with the engineers at Acheux.

Resting under canvas at Lealvillers George photographed John Ewing (left) and John Yarr (right). This photograph was taken at some time during late May or early June 1916.

1 JULY 1916

By mid-June 1916 preparations for the long awaited offensive were at an advanced stage. The Young Citizens were billeted in tents within Aveluy Wood on the opposite side of the River Ancre to Authuille and Thiepval Wood. They formed working parties on a daily basis to assist the Royal Engineers in digging the assembly trenches within Thiepval Wood which they would occupy just prior to the battle commencing. On the 19 June Brigade Order No 50 announced the details of the general offensive. The Young Citizen Volunteers were to attack in support of the 10th Battalion of the Royal Inniskilling Fusiliers (known as 'The Derrys') on the left flank of the Brigade area from Thiepval Wood, specifically the frontage between the trenches known as Inverness Street and where Elgin Avenue joined with Thurso Street trench. On the right flank the 9th Royal Inniskilling Fusiliers would be supported by the 11th Royal Inniskilling Fusiliers.

The day of the attack was designated as 'Z' day and was to be preceded by five days of artillery bombardment on U, V, W, X and Y days with U day being the 24 June,1916. The bombardment was intended to soften the German positions and destroy the barbed wire entanglements around their trenches while at the same time forcing the defenders, and in particular the machine-gunners, deep into their protective dugouts thus enabling the attacking forces to reach their trenches unhindered.

On the 23 June, the day before 'U' day, the YCVs were

ordered into Thiepval Wood and instructed to carry mortar shells from the main ammunition dump through the wood to the front line mortar positions. A total of 638 men formed an extended line to pass the shells from one to the other.

George photographed John Ewing engaged in this work in Thiepval Wood. He can be seen on the previous page with a mortar shell while resting at a junction between two communication trenches. The type of shell that John is seen holding, the two inch 'Toffee Apple' shell, was used to destroy and clear the German wire entanglements. In the photograph it can be seen to be fitted with a time delay fuse rather than an impact detonating fuse. The time delay fuse allowed the shell to penetrate deep into the wire entanglements before exploding, thus maximising the destructive effect. The shell's design and shape also meant that it would not penetrate the ground, exploding on the surface with greater wire-cutting effect.

This work continued all day and into the early morning; they did not leave Thiepval Wood until 3.45 am and had then to march to Headuville, some seven miles away. As they made their way out of Thiepval Wood just before dawn on Saturday the 24 June, the British bombardment of the German defensive positions commenced, marking the beginning of the offensive.

36th (Ulster) Divisional Order No 30 quite succinctly outlined the objective of the artillery bombardment as follows:

"The object of the bombardment is to kill as many of the enemy as possible, to blow in his trenches and machine-gun emplacements, to cut his wire, destroy his morale and pave the way for the infantry assault."

The Young Citizens remained at Headuville as the bombardment continued until they received orders to move again into Thiepval Wood and take up positions in the assembly trenches. This was now the late evening of 'X' day, (Tuesday) just over twenty-four hours from 'Z' day, (Thursday) the proposed starting day of the offensive. There is no doubt that tension among the men increased as the bombardment continued. The gravity of the situation was not lost on Sergeant Jimmy Scott. Although a veteran of the South African campaign he had not experienced such a bombardment. If he harboured feelings of fear and apprehension he may not have betrayed the same to the men of 'B' Company but we know for certain that at some point on the 27 June he felt the need to take time to write his will into the back of his Army pay book. The page in the book had remained blank until this date. The battalion made their way to Martinsart and prepared to move on to the trenches at Thiepval Wood. As they made the final preparations they received orders to return to Forceville as 'Z' day had been postponed for forty-eight hours. They had been brought to the brink and pulled back at the last hour. The attack was delayed until the morning of Saturday the 1 July 1916 at a time yet to be fixed.

One photograph (opposite top) that George Hackney takes at this time is titled simply 'Y'. In it we can see the view across the Ancre Valley from a position on the road between Authuille and Mesnil, known today as Mesnil-Martinsart. The position, just at the edge of Aveluy Wood, is close to an observation post used at the time by officers to observe the progress of the bombardment and in particular to assess the effectiveness of the shell-fire in destroying the enemy wire entanglements. The position can be easily found today and offers a commanding view of the right flank of the 36th Ulster Division sector just as it would have done a century ago. Today however, close to where Thiepval Village stood, the skyline is dominated by presence of the Thiepval Memorial to the Missing.

On the night of Friday the 30 June, following an improvement in the weather conditions which had been the cause of the 48 hour delay, the YCV battalion once again made its way across the River Ancre and into the assembly trenches at Thiepval Wood in preparation for the attack. At 2.30 am it was reported to headquarters that all men were in position. Zero hour had been set for 7.30 am. There was to be no more delay, the time had come. At 7.20 am the 10th Royal Inniskilling Fusiliers left the front line trenches and lay down in No-Man's-Land just short of the line of the British artillery barrage. The Young Citizen Volunteers moved up to the front line trenches vacated by the Inniskillings and waited for the final minutes to pass. On hearing the notes of the regimental call followed by 'the advance' sounded on the bugle merging into the shrill piercing call of the platoon commanders' whistles George Hackney, Jimmy Scott, John Ewing, Paul Pollock and all of the other Ulster men in the YCV battalion and many other units, mounted the parapet and marched into history.

From that moment, as the Adjutant, Captain Alan Mulholland commenced recording his account of the battle in the War Diary, until this day almost a century later, much has been written and spoken of the heroic deeds performed and the terrible losses endured by the Ulster Division on that misty July morning. Historians, diarists and journalists of the day have, over the years, described the advance in detail. However, in all of these accounts one element is missing – actual photographs taken during the battle.

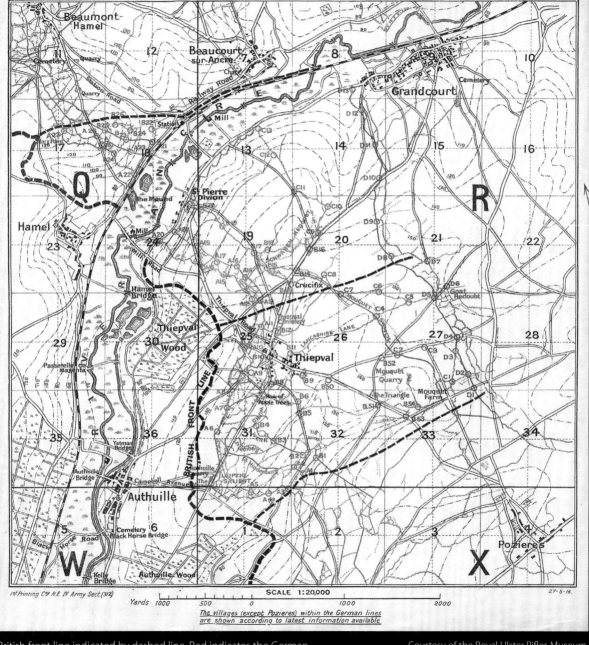

British front line indicated by dashed line. Red indicates the German
trenches with labels to identify the objectives for attacking forces.

Courtesy of the Royal Ulster Rifles Museum.

As the YCV battalion advanced it quickly became apparent that not all of the enemy machine-guns had been silenced. The Brigade level War Diary recorded that four guns were actively engaging the attacking forces from in and around the ruins of Thiepval village on the division's right flank. It was estimated that two of these guns were holding back the 32nd Division advance while another two swept across No-Man's-Land in front of Thiepval Wood and on the exposed right flank of the Ulster Division. George Hackney's 'B' Company exited the front line trenches at the left flank of the divisional boundary for the attack. Here the ground begins to slope down towards the Ancre. Once 'B' Company were clear of the Sunken Road they were sheltered from direct rifle and machine-gun fire from Thiepval village but were still exposed to fire from across the Ancre Valley around the area of Beaumont-Hamel.

The attacking battalions were to follow a compass bearing of 69 degrees from their starting positions at Thiepval Wood. The initial objective of the 109th Brigade was to take and hold a section of the 'C' line between point 'C8' on the right flank and a position between point 'C9' and 'C11' on the left. This meant that the infamous section of trench works known as the Schwaben Redoubt had to be over-run and held. The Schwaben Redoubt, up to this point, was thought to have been impregnable. Once these positions on the 'C' line were taken the attacking battalions were to hold and consolidate the position before sending an officer's reconnaissance patrol forward to the German 'D' line trench to ascertain the strength of the defending troops. Depending on the result of this reconnaissance the 107th Brigade were to move through the positions held by the 109th Brigade troops and attack the 'D' line after the defensive wire entanglements were destroyed by exploding

Bangalore torpedoes brought to the 'C' line during the consolidation phase, under the cover of a smoke barrage.

George Hackney's actions on the morning of the 1 July were nothing short of remarkable. For him, and the rest of his battalion on the left flank of the attack, for the first hour or so things went reasonably well. The attacking forces quickly took, cleared and fought through the first two German trench lines that formed the 'A' line. They then advanced towards the 'B' line and began bringing the necessary equipment forward to attempt to consolidate their positions around the 'C' line.

It was during these first few hours of the attack that George stepped out of his role as a soldier and decided to document events unfolding around him during the battle as a photographer. In viewing these images we must remember that these were not photographs taken by a photojournalist 'embedded' in a relatively safe area, nor were they posed or re-created later away from the battlefield. These images were taken during the battle by a combatant actually involved in the event – the event that was to become the British Army's worst day in its entire history.

On at least three occasions during this horrific battle George stopped, removed his 'Watch Pocket' camera from his pocket or pouch, extended the bellows, set his focus distance, aperture and shutter speed before framing and releasing the shutter to take a photograph. The three photographs that he took on that day can be regarded as decisive moments, not just in the photographic sense, but in recording moments when the battle took a particular turn, and on one occasion the photograph taken provides us with an insight into George's state of mind, and allows us to perhaps begin to understand how his experiences during the battle led him to take a particular turn of faith in his later years.

Perhaps the best general overview of the battle appears in the 36th (Ulster) Division's General Staff War Diary, which drew on intelligence from signals of all the brigades in the division and from observation points overlooking the battlefield and which later included reports on the battle. These official entries can help us identify the rough location on the battlefield from where and when the photographs may have been taken. In one such report Major-General Oliver Nugent himself records:

"8 am. By 8 am our troops were in possession of the S.W. side of the Schwaben Redoubt and the rest of the 'B' line up to B.19 was also in our hands."

He goes on to describe the attack to the north of the River Ancre, just across the valley from George's position and referred to as the "right bank" of the river:

"At 7.52 am a telephone message had been received from the 29th Division to the effect that the first objective had been taken. It appears that their leading troops reached the Station Road but that machine-guns were turned on them and supports were unable to reach them. At any rate at 8.03 am a report came in that the 29th Division had been repulsed and that the enemy had retaken his first line. No further progress was made with this attack on the right bank of the Ancre…"

With time and a rough position recorded in General Nugent's notes we can answer the 'where' and 'when' questions. The author positioned himself roughly between the positions known as 'B18' and 'B17' just south west of the Schwaben Redoubt (see map page 88). On the battle field today and using a lens with a similar field of view to that used by George, the skyline across the valley can be matched at the left and right edges of the frame thus giving a rough indication of where he was when he took

the photograph. George recorded that the photograph was taken "At the German third line on 1st July during attack". It is significant that he wrote that he was at the "third" line. He would of course have counted the trenches as he crossed them. The 'A' line , as referred to by the officers consisted of two lines of trenches, the 'B', 'C' and 'D' lines were made up of just a single trench line each. The third trench was therefore the 'B' line. It can be seen that the field boundaries today on the north side of the Ancre valley roughly match the zig-zag pattern of the original front line. The large farm buildings are built in the area of Hedgerow Avenue and Connantray Avenue trenches, the area from which George had previously photographed the German lines where he then found himself. This gives us an important clue as to why he took this particular scene. In his photograph it can be seen that a bombardment was taking place in and around the British front line positions,

positions where he had been just weeks earlier. This was significant enough for George, but perhaps this scene gave him the first indications of how events would turn. General Nugent had the benefit of all of the signals, intelligence and observers at his disposal to realise that the attack on the north slope of the Ancre Valley had failed. George could see with his own eyes that the attack had faltered. Had he realised then that when the German machine-guns south of Beaumont-Hamel and Station Road had repulsed the 9th Royal Irish Fusiliers and the 12th Royal Irish Rifles they would soon sweep the ground where he stood?

He then directed his attention to events closer at hand. Large parties of German soldiers had surfaced from their dugouts in the 'B' line trench and had begun to surrender to the Young Citizens. At this stage George could have been forgiven for thinking that the battle was almost won; the YCVs had so far achieved all of their objectives. They

had advanced through three lines of German trenches and were beginning the job of consolidating their positions prior to a final attack on the German 'D' line. With streams of defeated Germans emerging from the ground with arms raised in surrender George once again recorded the moment. In his photograph on the previous page taken from a position close to the ground, most likely looking over the rim of a shell crater, the German troops make their way along the skyline 'covered' by a Lewis gun team (left of image). Some of the attacking troops appear to have their rifles slung in an almost relaxed manner.

George took a second photograph (below) of the surrendering German troops from another location. Again, in this image we can see the line of enemy troops, arms raised, crossing the skyline. Two versions of this photograph exist however. In one (below right), printed in an album which he used to sell prints from after the war, all that can be seen is the line of surrendering prisoners. The original image however tells a different story for

in the foreground at the left of the frame George has photographed a dead German soldier. This inclusion places a completely different meaning to the photograph. In simplistic terms, in the original image George shows us his enemy, dead and close at hand. In the distance the defeated army surrendering to George's comrades, the friends he knew and trained with and who had made the transition from civilian to soldier along with him. Here they were, for a moment victorious in the first hours of the battle. They had carried out what was expected of them, all of the work, training and planning had paid off. What George was to quickly learn, as taught to officers and leaders since, was that no plan, however well conceived, survives contact with the enemy.

The tide was about to turn and George's attitude to the photograph changed with it. In his later years he had edited the photograph by cutting off the section that included the dead German soldier. We can only speculate as to why but most probably his experiences later that day eroded the

BELUM.Y15513, Photograph © National Museums Northern Ireland, Collection Ulster Museum

thought process that made him take the original scene. By the end of the 1 July 1916 George had simply become a different man, scarred physically and mentally by what he had witnessed. He took no more photographs that day.

General Nugent records the moment the tide turned in his report on the battle:

"The position at this time was undoubtedly serious. North of the Ancre the attack had failed; on our right Thiepval was untaken. Both flanks were in the air, and machine-guns from St Pierre Divion, Thiepval and Beaucourt Redoubt were playing havoc with the troops. This position was represented to Corps at 8.32 am and again at 8.54 am."

There is evidence that the men of the Young Citizen Volunteers carried out their orders almost to the letter. In a statement recorded from Rifleman George Courtney on the 7 September 1916 while he was convalescing at his home at 25 Wimbledon Street in Belfast, he recounts the actions of Captain Charles Owen Slacke of Wheatfield House in Belfast:

"On the first day of July last at 7.30 o'clock a.m. we received orders to advance and occupy the third line of German trenches at Thiepval Wood, France and there to await further orders. Captain Slacke led the attack and he and the majority of the men advancing succeeded in reaching the objective when he told the men (of whom I was one) to remain where we were until he gave us further orders. He and Lieutenants Gracey and Robb and two officers of the 'Inniskillings' whose names I do not know then proceeded to the fourth line of German trenches where I saw them in conversation. During this time the Germans were firing their machine-guns.

Our sergeant saw that Captain Slacke had been slightly wounded and he passed the information down the line. I saw Captain Slacke and his servant – I think Bennet is the name of the latter – returning to where we were – namely the third line of German trenches – on his way back to the dressing station (the Germans were at that time heavily shelling their first and second lines of trenches which were occupied by our reinforcements consisting of the 8th and 9th Royal Irish Rifles). He passed to the second line of German trenches and from thence towards the first line. Shortly after he left the second line I saw a high explosive shell from the German guns fall about where he was and after the smoke cleared away I looked – as I was anxious about him – if I could see any signs of him but I could not. Therefore I concluded that he had been blown to pieces. The time would be to the best of my recollection between ten and eleven o'clock a.m."

Captain Slacke, brother-in-law to Sir Thomas Dixon, was initially recorded as missing in action. His remains were remarkably recovered in November 1917 by a burial party and were eventually laid to rest in Connaught Cemetery in front of Thiepval Wood.

By late morning and early afternoon on the 1 July 1916 the Ulster Division found itself exposed and under attack from three sides. A fact that often escapes visitors to the battlefield today is the actual distance covered by the men of the Ulster Division during the battle. The distance from the starting point at the British front line trench in Thiepval Wood to the German 'C' line is approximately 1½ kilometres and the distance to the 'D' line, over two kilometres at places. Sergeant Jim Maultsaid of the YCV battalion described the turning point of the battle later in his account:

"I was not long in the fourth line until our troops who had captured the fifth began to fall back as the German counter attack had now been launched against us in our new position taken from them early in the morning. It was a masterly retirement and every inch of the ground was contested but sheer weight of numbers beat us slowly back. Our rifle and machine-gun fire, not to mention the effective work of our artillery assisted by batteries of French 7's played havoc with the advancing hordes of Germans who tried to retake their lost positions. We had to clear out of fourth line and move back to a shallow trench we had dug early that day, a little in advance of their old third line."

Sergeant Jimmy Scott's only account of the battle, passed by word of mouth to his wife and then down through three generations, to his sons, grandsons and eventually great-grandson simply states: "We were left out on our own, we had to fight a rear guard action to get back."

And fight they did, through the long July day and into the night. As dawn broke on the morning of the 2 July it was realised that a section of German trenches was still being held by the Ulstermen in the area of points 'B17', 'A16', 'A18' and 'A19'. These positions were held until the morning of the 3 July when what remained of the 36th (Ulster) Division was finally relieved by the 49th Division.

At 2.00 pm on the 2 July what remained of the 14th Battalion of the Royal Irish Rifles (YCV) was formally relieved from reserve positions in Thiepval Wood. Out of a battalion of around 860 officers and men only two officers, Lieutenants Monard and Hogg, led 120 men back across the South Causeway over the River Ancre to Martinsart Wood where they fell, exhausted.

The men George had photographed in happy, often mischievous poses, were all gone. Most were killed or missing but even those who remained were not the same men they had been. They had become witnesses to death and destruction beyond description.

Jimmy Scott had for the time being, survived another battle. He was promoted to Company Sergeant Major in charge of 'C' Company. John Yarr had been shot in the right foot and was evacuated from the front. John Ewing survived the battle and was promoted to Corporal with effect from the 1 July. James Fitzsimmons was awarded the Military Medal for gallantry and promoted to Sergeant. His brother Jack was killed in action attempting to carry a signal back to headquarters across No-Man's-Land. John Hunter and Paul Pollock, who had shared his Christmas parcel with the platoon at Pernois, were both missing, believed killed in action.

George Hackney was promoted to acting Corporal rank on the 1 July. He remained with the YCV battalion until the 7 July when he was admitted to a field Hospital at a requisitioned farmstead called Val de Maison outside Puchevillers. His physical injuries were not serious and indeed, the hospital at Val de Maison had been designated as a rest station. A facility where only men whom it was thought could recover within 10 days were sent. George had however suffered deeper psychological wounds, the scars of which remained with him into his latter years.

General Nugent's final estimate of the casualties for the 1 July operation, as entered in the General Staff War Diary was as follows:

The total were:-
107th Brigade, 76 Officers and 1360 OR's (Other Ranks)
108th Brigade, 69 Officers and 1980 OR's
109th Brigade, 69 Officers and 1870 OR's

Added together, along with numbers from the Royal Artillery and the 16th Royal Irish Rifles (Pioneers), the total casualties for the 36th (Ulster) Division were recorded as 216 Officers and 5266 men. Of the casualties in the 109th Brigade, those from the 14th Royal Irish Rifles (YCV) amounted to 16 Officers and 300 'other ranks'.

At Val de Maison George returned to his photography and took a picture of a group of survivors of the battle preparing food outside the main building. The farm, although renovated slightly, still exists today and shows signs of having been used as a hospital during the Napoleonic wars and also during World War Two.

The remaining survivors of the 14th Royal Irish Rifles (YCV) made their way over the week following the battle to Candas, close to where George was recuperating. There they boarded a military train which brought them eventually to their next sector of the front line, Red Lodge and Ploegsteert near Messines in Belgium. Here, on the 23 July 1916 they moved into position in support of the 9th Inniskilling Fusiliers and the 12th Royal Irish Rifles, the battalions that were attempting to advance north of the River Ancre on the 1 July when George took the photograph of the bombardment taking place across the valley.

BELGIUM: PLOEGSTEERT AND RED LODGE

On the 23 July 1916 George left the rest hospital at Val de Maison and set off on the journey to Belgium to rejoin his battalion. He eventually found the Young Citizen Volunteers on the 3 August in trenches at the Ploegsteert sector of the line close to Messines in Belgium. While pleased to see his old friends he was shocked to discover how few of the original battalion remained.

He resumed his photography over what would be his final weeks on the front line. The photographs he took were perhaps a welcome distraction and included mostly shots of original YCV men, survivors of the 1 July battle, the men he had trained with and knew from Belfast. Of all of the photographs he took while in France and Belgium those that were taken in the Red Lodge and Ploegsteert sectors are by far the best in terms of quality, exposure and composition. One can almost imagine him making his way along the trenches, meeting his old friends, perhaps for the first time since the battle, and photographing them as they exchange tales of that awful event.

On the one hand he was photographing his mates; on the other he was documenting the lives of those men who survived. In the wake of the great tide of loss that had swept over the battalion I believe he realised the importance of his photography to those who remained and to the families and loved ones of the fallen.

George's first task on arrival with the battalion was to collect all of his mail which had been sent to the battalion while he was at Val de Maison. His first photograph (opposite) taken in the area shows us the field post office, managed by the signals section. Signalling wire can be seen coiled up on the ground and secured on barbed wire spigots. The mail sacks can also be seen hanging from a branch on the left and the tent upright on the right. George named the man seated on the right of the photograph as Corporal John Harrip.

John Wesley Harrip was born in Cookstown in 1885. In 1903 he joined the Northern Bank and was employed as a bank clerk. He transferred to various positions over the following ten years or so including posts at Head Office in Belfast, and branches at Clones, Downpatrick, Newry, Londonderry and also in Dublin. On enlisting with the 14th Royal Irish Rifles in July 1914 he was 29 years old and gave his address as Togherdoo, Dromore, County Tyrone. John served with the Young Citizen Volunteers until the battalion was disbanded when he was transferred to the 16th Royal Irish Rifles, the division's pioneer or combat engineer battalion. He survived the war and was discharged from the army on the 7 February 1919. He then returned to his civilian occupation, taking up a post with the Northern Bank again at their head office. In 1940 he was appointed manager of the Connswater branch in East Belfast. At the time of his retirement from the Bank in 1947 he lived at Massey Park in the Belmont area of the east of the city.

After collecting and reading his mail George sought out a soldier whom he had learned had been close to Paul Pollock on the day of the 1st July battle in an attempt to glean any information that might shed some light on what happened to Paul. This turned out to be a fruitless task. On the 3 August he wrote in his diary:

"The part of the line where we now are seems very quiet and it's well because we certainly have not recovered from our 1st July experience. I had no duty to do tonight so had only to 'stand to' after which I hunted a chap who had been with Paul in the attack. But unfortunately his information was not of much

value. Towards the end of our conversation our guns started to fire so we parted as I wanted to get back to my own part of the line in case Fritz started retaliation but he didn't and I was not at all sorry, so I got a chance of sleeping during the night."

During early August in a front line dugout at Ploegsteert George photographed two men (opposite). They were, at the rear, William John (Gus) Reid who came from 6 New North Queen Street in Belfast and in front of him, reading the *Daily Sketch* is Joseph John Johnston of 30 Coolbeg Street in Belfast. Gus Reid was to die only a year later, killed in action on the 16 August 1917 during the Battle of Langemark. Joe Johnston had been wounded on the 1 July and had only just returned to the battalion himself when the photograph was taken. He was later transferred to the Machine Gun Corps and survived the war.

In the photograph a sign directs "Keep down", a serious direction clearly not to be ignored as just above the sign can be seen ripped and punctured sand bags, undoubtedly caused by enemy fire.

Above the dugout entrance we can see a blind which would have been made out of an old blanket, or similar absorbent material, placed on top of a waterproof sheet. The purpose of this blind was not just to keep out the weather, it had a much more important purpose and that was to act as a form of gas proofing

for the dugout. The blanket was sprayed with a chemical, known to the troops as 'Hypo Solution' kept in rum jars inside the doorway. The waterproof sheet was rolled up with the impregnated blanket to keep the blanket damp and prevent the Hypo Solution from evaporating, ensuring it stayed effective. Ideally the blanket and waterproof cover were rolled up across the entrance on a wooden stick roller and held by a string tied in a slip knot. In the event of a gas attack the knot was pulled and the cover released to fall to the ground. It was then laced closed at the sides and sealed at ground level by pushing the stick into a small, pre-dug furrow and holding it in position with earth. Gas entering the dugout would have to pass through the Hypo Solution which neutralised it. The use of this type of gas proof door covering did not obviate the necessity for the occupants to wear their gas helmets during an attack.

Again in the Ploegsteert sector during early August 1916 George photographed Sergeant Hubert Jones standing in a front line trench (left). Hubert was one of two brothers serving in the battalion. He lived at 9 Little Victoria Street in Belfast. As a member of 'B' Company he rose swiftly through the ranks. At the time George took the photograph he would have been a Sergeant for only about two weeks, having been promoted on the 27 July 1916. Hubert went on to become a Company Sergeant Major in the YCV battalion before obtaining a commission into the 12th Royal Irish Rifles in June 1918. He was killed in action just two weeks before the end of the war during an attack on retreating German units east of Courtrai on the 25 October 1918. He was 25 years old at the time of his death.

George's next subject in the Ploegsteert sector was Sergeant Sam Martin (below). He also was photographed in the front line. We can see in the series of Ploegsteert trench photographs that the trenches were not actually dug into the ground, rather they were built upwards in the form of sandbag walls. This was due to the topography of the area. The land was particularly low lying and waterlogged which meant that digging became impractical as any trench dug into the ground would quickly fill with water. Typically the positions were built up using sandbags with wooden slatted 'duck boards' on the ground usually covering a drainage trench. We can see that design of trench clearly in this photograph. The fire-step is a constructed wooden bench as opposed to an actual step cut into the earth at the bottom of the trench as was evident in the Thiepval Wood photographs.

Sam Martin was born in Belfast in 1890. At the outbreak of war he lived at 28 Thalia Street in the city with his parents and brother, Herbert Martin. Both men enlisted in the 14th Royal Irish Rifles but Herbert transferred shortly after to the 16th (Pioneer) Battalion of the Royal Irish Rifles. Before the war Sam had worked as a clerk in the John Shaw Brown Linen

Mill at Edenderry Village outside Belfast. His book keeping skills were discovered and put to use as Sam was initially employed as assistant company accountant with lance corporal rank. He moved up the ranks and was promoted to Sergeant on the 1 July 1916. Sam left the battalion on the 15 February 1917 for officer training at Cadet School and obtained a commission in the 8th Queen's (Royal West Surrey) Regiment on the 31 July 1917.

As Sam was joining his new battalion as an officer he was informed of the death of his brother, Herbert. Just five days earlier Herbert was employed in clearing a channel from the Moat to the Railway trench at Ypres in Belgium. The work had taken two days and had to be frequently halted due to heavy gas shell bombardments. Herbert was killed during one of these bombardments along with his officer and four other men.

Sam Martin continued on as 2nd Lieutenant in 'B' Company of the 8th Queen's. By mid March 1918 his battalion were operating in the Le Verger area of France about eight miles or so north west of St Quentin. Rather than hold a continuous line of trenches the line at this point had been broken and consolidated into a number of fortified strongpoints. Lieutenant Martin's 'B' Company had been divided into four in order to man each of the four strongpoints north east of the village of Le Vergnier, named Pieumel Post, Orchard Post, Fort Bell and Fort Dyce.

On the morning of the 21 March at 4.30 am an intense bombardment rained onto the British positions. As dawn broke a thick fog covered the lines which concealed a large scale German attack, what was to be known as the Kaiserschlacht or 'Emperor's Battle'. The forts and strong points were quickly surrounded and cut off from the rest of the battalion, their occupants unable to see and engage their enemy, After two days of fighting the occupants were forced to surrender as their positions were overrun. Sam was taken prisoner along with many others along the front and moved to a prisoner of war camp in Germany. His mother Annie, now widowed and mourning the death of one son and desperate for news of the other, placed an appeal for information regarding Sam's whereabouts in the *Belfast Telegraph* stating that he was missing in action.

Sam was uninjured when taken prisoner and survived the last eight months of the war in captivity. Following the armistice in November 1918 he was released and repatriated, arriving at Hull on the SS *Pofta* on the 29 November before returning to Belfast. In 1922 when his medals were finally sent to him he was still living with his mother at 28 Thalia Street, off the Donegal Road in Belfast.

As George continued his familiarisation of the front line positions he took two photographs of a position identified by a marker board as 'Trench 131'. This type of board,

which faced away from the enemy, was used to help aircraft pilots navigate as they flew across the lines. The numbers corresponded to positions marked on the trench maps issued at the time. In this case Trench 131 ran close to a ruined, moated farm known as Seaforth Farm. A modern farm has been built close to the site of the original and until recently part of the moat remained. It has now been filled in.

In the second photograph, overleaf, we can see the moat filled with water and the '131' sign just visible in the distance. The devastation is clear evidence of this area's front line location.

On the 26 August 1916, a few days after George took these photographs, Rifleman Samuel Athay, a new reinforcement from Saffron Road, Whitehall in Bristol, was killed when, at 10.30 in the morning, two enemy shells exploded in the trench. Samuel had only joined the battalion on the 13 July 1916, some five weeks earlier.

In the next striking image we see Samuel Stansfield on the left with John Dixon on the right. These men were part of the Lewis Gun team and were photographed in the front line at Messines. Sam Stansfield, originally from Dunluce Avenue in Belfast was commissioned in the Royal Irish Fusiliers on the 29 October 1918, just days before the end of the war. He survived the war and later lived in Banbridge.

John Harvey Dixon was one of two brothers who served in the YCV battalion. They lived at 75 Ormeau Road in Belfast. John's brother Ben was wounded on the 3 May 1916 at Thiepval and at the time this photograph was taken he was at home in Belfast suffering from the effects of shell shock. John Dixon was a valued member of 'B' Company who had distinguished himself with his skill in using the Lewis machine-gun during the battle of Whytschaete on the 7 June 1917. John Ewing later described him as being "pretty handy with the LG [Lewis gun]" in a letter written to George. John Dixon was killed in action on the 16 August 1917 at Langemark; his body was never found.

On returning to the YCV battalion George had been detailed orderly duties with the occasional spell spent on working parties repairing the sandbag trench works and carrying up supplies to the front line at night. It became apparent to him that he could not perform at the level that he once could. He may not have realised it but it appears that he was suffering from the effects of the trauma he had

experienced during the battle at Thiepval the previous month. He began to make mistakes.

On the 14 August he was reported by the Regimental Sergeant Major for allowing a working party under his charge to loiter between jobs. The disciplinary action was initially halted by his captain, Thomas Mayes, who looked into the matter, discovering that the party had completed

their work quickly, buying time for the quick cup of tea they were drinking when the Sergeant Major passed by. George's colleagues must have noticed a change in him. Gus Reid allowed him to sleep in on the following morning, their first day in the Red Lodge sector, obviously sensing that his friend needed rest. It was later that day that George appeared before the Commanding Officer to answer for his offence of "allowing his men to loiter". It appears that Captain Mayes may have had a word with the Commanding Officer because the charge was quashed.

On the night of the 17 August George was detailed on a working party to repair a trench parapet. He wrote in his diary:

> "I was immediately warned off for a working party at 8.00 to the trenches. When we reached our destination – the front line – we were told that the parapet was to be thickened so we had to go outside to do so and I must confess my nerves were hard to keep under control especially when we heard a German Machine Gun firing above our heads but particularly once when he started plugging the bullets in the bank not a couple of yards from where we were. If I ever hugged Mother Earth I did it on this occasion. Fortunately he did not get one of us altho' there were 20 of us all close together, a lovely target. We duly finished the job about 12.30 am and I felt more satisfied when I had got back into the trench."

It was in the Red Lodge sector where George took his last three photographs in Belgium. These were taken in and around the British reserve line positions which had been dug into a slope that formed part of the Rosenberg family chateau and estate outside Messines. The individual dugouts took the form of wooden huts sited on the sloping woodland, out of sight from the enemy positions. The men called the huts 'dog kennels' due to their general appearance. The officers were billeted in pre-fabricated wooden huts, similar to large garden sheds.

George took a photograph (opposite) of his two old friends John Ewing, on the right, and Joe Johnston sitting in one of the dog kennels. Both men look quite serious in their demeanour, perhaps concerned at the change they have noticed in their friend's behaviour or maybe concerned about his future. They too of course had been through the battle on the 1st July and would have had their own traumatic experiences to reflect on. They were no longer the happy band of men making their way through France larking and joking. They had been to hell and back with only the prospect of more to come.

In the distance, on the skyline can be seen an odd pointed structure. This is a building, undoubtedly part of the Rosenberg estate, which had possibly been used for hunting or the curing of game. It was used as the post for the battalion gas guard, placed in a forward position where the occupants could raise the alarm if gas was released and the wind was blowing towards their positions. George did his spell of duty there and photographed the curious looking building with its raised roof.

By the 21 August George had made up his mind. He had been continually unwell and lethargic and appeared to be suffering from the effects of stress. He went to see Captain Mayes after breakfast:

> "Rose before 9.00. After breakfast and got Mr Mayes to censor a parcel for me to send home after which I

got it packed up and duly handed in. Went on sick parade on account of my nerves but was given M&D [Medicine and Duty]. Paraded at 2.30 pm to take over a Bomb Store Guard, so our Company was due for Reserve this time so I happened to fall in lucky as it wasn't so bad on my nerves as Working Parties."

We can only speculate on what the package was that he referred above to but it was most likely his camera and undeveloped material. Even being caught in possession of a camera was deemed a serious offence against military law which carried a sentence of imprisonment. If George had planned to pass through the casualty system he would have known that his camera would in all likelihood be detected and confiscated. Captain Mayes, who we know had been sympathetic to George's photography in the past may have facilitated its safe passage home.

George photographed Captain Mayes (below, seated) and two other unidentified officers outside the officers mess, 'Holy Flip Shack' at Red Lodge. This photograph of the officer's quarters is interesting for another reason: the box

at the left of the frame had 'Fortnum & Mason, Piccadilly London' written on the front. It became almost customary for officers to open an account at Fortnum's and have what became known as a 'Chop Box' sent out to them at the front line. Such a box could have contained almost anything but generally it was sweets, preserves, meats, delicacies and fine wines, things that couldn't otherwise be found at the front. One entire floor at Fortnum and Mason's store in London became dedicated to the preparation and delivery of the officer's chop boxes.

It was realised that certain items did not travel well, for instance bread which invariably did not reach the troops in a fresh and edible form, so the officers made do with Dundee Cake instead, which was delivered in a tin. Fortnum's also supplied items of uniform for officers, made to order. Interestingly we can see that Captain Mayes is wearing what appears to be a particularly fine pair of leather riding boots, most likely ordered from Fortnum's catalogue and delivered to the front.

Photographs of the huts at Red Lodge are very rare, in fact this may be the only one remaining in existence. Photographs of a Fortnum and Mason 'Chop Box' at the front line are also rare. To find both subjects in one photograph is exceptional.

A week after reporting to Captain Mayes George reported sick a second time owing to his 'nerves'. On this occasion he was examined and sent to hospital. On the 30 August 1916 George's war effectively ended. Although he did not know it, he had just begun his journey home.

His France and Belgium album ended with the inclusion of a photograph of the grave of a Young Citizen Volunteer. Rifleman Joseph Sloane, a fellow 'B' Company member, had been injured during the build up to the 1 July attack and had been sent to hospital on the same day as George himself. Joseph rejoined the battalion a week earlier than George on the 16 July 1916 and was killed while on a working party at trenches at the Grande Munque Farm sector three weeks later on the 6 August 1916. He originally came from Ballygawley, County Tyrone and later lived at Donnybrook Street in Belfast with his widowed mother, Jane. He was 25 years old when he died.

PEACE

On the 1 September 1916, George was examined by a doctor at the Divisional Rest Station. He was handed a card marked 'Neurasthenia and DAH' and was then told that he was "going down the line" to the Casualty Clearing Station at Balieul. DAH stood for Disordered Action of the Heart. These were diagnostic terms given to patients who were suffering from a range of symptoms which we refer to now as 'shell shock'. As the war progressed military physicians were increasingly reluctant to use the term and diagnosed patients, like George, using a number of different forms of terminology such as, 'functional disorder', 'hysteria', 'neurasthenia', and 'neurosis'. Today, many of the symptoms experienced by such patients may be attributed to what we now know to be 'Post Traumatic Stress Disorder' or PTSD.

George, in spite of his condition, was fortunate in receiving his diagnosis when he did. A few weeks later, on the 14 October 1916, having been forced to issue a directive owing to the increasing number of men reporting ill with symptoms similar to George's, orders were issued by the Adjutant General, Major General George Henry Fowke in the following terms:

"Those who when engaged with the enemy fail to maintain equilibrium do so either –
Because they are lacking the nerve and stability which must be assumed to be inherent in all soldiers, or –

Because they have been subject to some extraordinary exposure not incidental to all military operations.

Those who have committed themselves for the first of the above reasons cannot be allowed to escape disciplinary action on the ground of a medical diagnosis of 'Shell Shock' or 'Neurasthenia' or 'Inability to stand shell-fire'.

It has too often happened that officers and men who have failed in their duty have used such expressions to describe their state of non-effectiveness, and medical officers without due consideration of the military issues at stake have accepted such cases as being in the same category as ordinary illness."

General Fowke went on to state in the same report:

"It should be for a Court Martial to decide whether the evidence as to the existence of actual disease is such as to justify absolving an offender from penal consequence."

Fowke concluded:

"Nerve failure believed to belong to the second class of cases, those due to extraordinary exposure, should not be classified as a wound on medical authority alone.

The diagnosis 'Shell Shock Wound' should in no case be made until the evidence of the Commanding Officer or soldier affected has been obtained that his condition originated immediately upon his being exposed to the effects of a specific explosion."

Reading these orders one has to wonder how any soldier at Thiepval on the 1 July 1916, or in any battle of the Great War for that matter, could be expected to gather evidence of the cause of his illness being attributable to a single specific explosion.

On the 13 September 1916, exactly two years from the date he enlisted, George was driven by motor ambulance to the docks at Calais where he boarded the ship which took him to England. His relief at being evacuated to safety is evident in the account he recorded in his diary, the last line of which gives us an indication of the precautions he took in sending his camera and photographs ahead of him in order to avoid confiscation and the censor:

"We reached Dover at 12.55 pm I shall never forget the thrill that passed through me – it was a hazy day – when the white cliff loomed into view and when we got within half-a-mile of the harbour I thought I had never seen so beautiful a view in my life before. The sun was shining through the haze and the cliffs were shaded from pure white to a rich golden and the water was a very vivid green. The beauty of the scene enchanted me and I felt full of regret when the boat brought us into harbour however the thought of having arrived in Dear Old England once more made up for me being taken away from the lovely picture. I longed to have my camera but perhaps its

just as well I hadn't it as I don't think I could have resisted the temptation to take a photo and I might have got into trouble as a result."

George boarded a train at Dover, his destination, Wharncliffe War Hospital in Sheffield. Wharncliffe had previously been known as the South Yorkshire Asylum, Wadsley, until the spring of 1915 when it underwent a conversion before being handed over to the War Office as a military hospital in April of that year.

From this point on George's life slowly began to return to normal. On the 3 October he received a visit from his brother William, who was serving as a merchant seaman. It appears, from George's diary notes, that William brought him his precious camera as his photography resumes the next day. George benefitted from various visits by old friends that he had known from his Co-Operative Holiday Society days who lived nearby, in and around Sheffield. Although a tonic for his recovery, the people George wanted to see more than anyone else were those at home in Belfast. On the 6 October George summoned the courage to make a request via the ward sister, Sister Ensell, for home leave. His request was forwarded to the hospital doctor, Major Gillespie and after a formal interview he was granted three days leave.

Between the 11–15 November 1916 George was on 'home leave'. He travelled via Manchester where he was met by his brother William, and they both made the sailing from Fleetwood to Belfast together. At 5.30 am George rose to discover that the ship had come to a halt. He quickly dressed and went up on deck only to find that they were held at anchor off Grey Point near Bangor at the entrance to Belfast Lough. He spent an agonising further wait of over five hours before finally docking at Belfast at mid-day. At 1.00 pm on the 12 October he walked through the door of his house, 'Portlean', on the Lansdowne Road in Belfast.

George continued with his treatment at Wharncliffe Hospital until he was moved back to Ireland and attached to the 18th Battalion of the Royal Irish Rifles based at Ballykinlar in County Down. With the absence of his service record, exact dates and details of his postings and medical condition cannot be accurately known but by examining the correspondence sent to him, in particular those letters from his old pal John Ewing and the steady stream of letters from Ernie McClatchey a picture can be built up.

By June 1917 he had been granted 'Permanent Home Duties' status due to the extent of his illness. He was then transferred to the Labour Corps around March 1918 as by that stage his original Young Citizen Volunteers battalion had been disbanded. By all accounts George finished his service in an office role attached to a Labour Corps Battalion based at Salisbury in England.

Many of the men he had served alongside had obtained commissions and were serving as officers. John Ewing finished the war as a Lieutenant in the London Irish Rifles, appointed just weeks before the war ended. Many more of course were killed or missing. George was kept up to date with events by John Ewing's letters and he regularly received greetings and good wishes from his old friends. There was no evidence that any of them harboured any resentful feelings towards him on account of his securing a 'handy turn' at home. It appears as if those who were there knew what he had been through and accepted that he had carried out his duty, was ill and deserved the rest he received.

Sad tidings were also conveyed by John in his letters. As the YCV battalion became engaged in more and more offensives the list of those who would not be returning grew ever longer. In one such letter dated the 12 February 1917, clearly in response to an enquiry by George, John Ewing described how the author's great-grandfather, George's old sergeant, Company Sergeant Major Jimmy Scott was killed in action:

"I am very glad to hear George that the doctor has assured you that you will recover, but, I hope it won't mean active service, at least I wouldn't think so for you wouldn't be right here until you would crack again. Yes it was very sad about Jimmy Scott. We had just relieved and he went into the dugout for something when a shell went clean through killing him immediately."

Jimmy Scott, the Boer War veteran, and ex-Royal Irish Fusilier, was killed at around 6.00 pm on the evening of the 22 January 1917 on the British front line opposite the German positions at Messines, just forward of a position known as Gabion Farm. The location today lies in the shadow of the Ireland Peace Tower. His men recovered his body from the ruined dugout and carried him for a mile along the communication trench known as 'Currie Avenue' through 'Gooseberry farm' and 'Stinking Farm' to his final resting place at La Plus Douve Farm Cemetery. There he was buried with full military honours in a service conducted by the Reverend James Gilbert Paton MC who was originally from Coleraine. The adjutant, Captain Alan Mulholland, who at that time was effectively in command of the YCV battalion wrote to Jane Scott, Jimmy's widow:

"I regret very much the loss of Sergeant-Major Scott. He was one of my best sergeant-majors, always bright and cheerful, a brave soldier and a great loss to the battalion."

Signaller William McCormack also recorded the loss in his diary:

"Left for trenches and got the length of 'Stinking Farm' A1. But from that onwards Fritz was peppering the line and communication trenches pretty heavily… two of the 9th got lovely 'blighty' ones and I was that much fed up that I was wishing for one myself, but no such luck. Anyhow I got the length of the front line A1, whilst Fritz, to celebrate the Kaisers birthday, continued to give us a jolly time of it and, unfortunately SM Scott was killed. He was very popular and it was a sore loss to the battalion."

Jimmy Scott was 35 years old when he died. Jane was left with five young children back in their home at Elm Street in Belfast.

Among the Ulster Museum's Hackney collection are two interesting photographs relating to Jimmy Scott. In the first (right) he can be seen standing in La Plus Douve Farm cemetery in Belgium at the grave of Bertie Joseph McCann.

McCann was a young Royal Irish Rifles lieutenant from Ballymena who had been killed on the 14 November 1916. He had originally enlisted with the Connaught Rangers before transferring to the Munster Fusiliers, part of the 10th Irish Division. With the 'Munsters' he fought at Suvla Bay during the Gallipoli campaign and after being wounded there was brought home for treatment.

On recuperation he applied for a commission and after attending Cadet School he was promoted to Second Lieutenant in the 18th (Reserve) Battalion of the Royal Irish Rifles before being attached to the 13th Royal Irish Rifles. At the time of his death his battalion was operating in the same sector as the YCV.

BELUM.Y15428, Photograph © National Museums Northern Ireland, Collection Ulster Museum

The second of the two photographs was also taken at La Plus Douve Farm. It showed Jimmy Scott's own grave. Remarkably, and by a strange turn of fate, Jimmy was buried in the same cemetery in January 1917, just a few weeks after being photographed there while paying his respects to Bertie McCann. This second photograph showed Jimmy's grave shortly after his interment with snow still lying on the ground. Another feature is the lines of trees that can be seen in the distance. The photograph appears to have been taken from a low angle, not from a standing position, giving it a similar appearance to the first photograph in which Jimmy appears. This may indicate that the same photographer took both photographs and was attempting to take the second in a similar manner to the first. The identity of the photographer is not known although one theory, based on the letters of George Hackney's photographic supplier Ernie McClatchey, suggests that it may have been John Ewing using George Hackney's first camera.

The Young Citizen Volunteers continued fighting in Flanders, distinguishing themselves in action during the battle for Whytschaete on the 7 June 1917 and suffering great loss in August 1917 during the battle of Langemark ahead of their disbandment in February 1918. George was kept updated by correspondence sent by a number of old friends but mostly by John Ewing who wrote to him on a regular basis with news from the front lines.

George continued to recover and was eventually discharged from Wharncliffe Hospital in June 1917 when he returned to Ireland attached to the 18th (Reserve) Battalion of the Royal Irish Rifles based at Ballykinlar in County Down. Men who had previously been injured would have normally 'passed through' the 18th Battalion to be re-trained and brought back to a suitable level of fitness and training before being sent back to the front lines.

By June 1918 George had been transferred from Ballykinlar to Salisbury Plain where he was attached to a Labour Corps Battalion. Here he remained until the end of the war, employed in office and orderly duties after being deemed to be unfit for front line active service. He was eventually discharged from the army on the 6 March 1919. He returned home to an island that had suffered the loss of over 49,000 men. The 36th (Ulster) Division alone by the end of the war had suffered 31,000 men killed, wounded or missing.

After the war ended George returned to Belfast and gradually slipped back into civilian life. Little is known of him during the post war years other than he continued to live in Belfast and regularly attended St Enoch's Presbyterian Church whose members had faithfully supported him before, during and after the war. In return George devoted a large amount of his time and energies to church life and, as a highly respected member he was ordained as a Church Elder in 1931.

Above: BELUM.Y15440, Photograph © National Museums Northern Ireland, Collection Ulster Museum

We do know that George did not continue his photography in any professional capacity and his photographs were, for the most part of the post-war years, kept away from public view. George learnt another skill that ultimately would lead to his life taking a completely different turn.

In 1913 a sixty year old masseur called Cunningham Witherow set up a practice at 95 Great Victoria Street in Belfast, having moved there from County Donegal. Cunningham continued to practice physiotherapy through the war years and established a reputation as a master of the profession, reported to have 'a magic touch', being particularly successful in his treatment of rheumatism. Cunningham moved to premises at 86 Dublin Road in Belfast and it was here that George went to him for treatment. During the course of the treatment George befriended Cunningham and eventually underwent an apprenticeship, becoming a masseur in his own right. George began to build up his own reputation, especially among the congregation at St Enoch's and when Cunningham Witherow passed away in his late eighties in 1939 George took over the business and continued to practice at the Dublin Road premises well into the 1950s.

It wasn't until 1956 that we can say with any certainty that his photographs were viewed in public. A pilgrimage to the old front lines in France and Belgium was organised by the Royal Ulster Rifles Association to take place to commemorate the 40th anniversary of the Battle of the Somme. By 1956 most of the veterans were in their sixties with their numbers falling as the years progressed. Prior to the visit various fundraising events were held to fund the trip. One such fundraising effort involved the showing of a set of lantern slides that included George Hackney's photographs and the later YCV photographs that were possibly taken by John Ewing along with the sketches of Jim Maultsaid. One known venue for the slide show was Cullybackey British Legion Hall in County Antrim. It was most likely at this time when George edited his 1 July photograph (page 92) before including it in his album.

In 1956 George Hackney joined the pilgrimage party when, on the 28 June he once again formed up 'in column of fours' at Belfast City Hall with a handful of YCVs amongst the eighty or so veterans, representatives of the twelve complete Royal Irish Rifles battalions who had fought on the 1 July forty years previously. The veterans laid wreaths at the Cenotaph at Belfast City Hall before marching to the Heysham Boat. The men eventually landed at Ostende in Belgium and they then travelled to Ypres, the now rebuilt city, very different from the rubble they once knew it to be. The old soldiers toured a number of the old battlefields before moving on to Arras and then, on the morning of the 1 July, forty years to the day, they faced Thiepval Ridge once more. An account of the pilgrimage in the 1956 edition of *Quis Separabit*, the regimental journal, describes the moment:

"Early on the morning of Sunday, 1st July 1956 these same men set off for Thiepval Ridge, by a vastly different route and method to that traversed by them exactly 40 years before. It was quite evident from the attitude of many that thoughts were far in the distant past as the convoy of buses laboured in first gear up the notorious "Sunken Road" of unhappy memories, now quite a pleasant place compared with the cauldron of hell it was in 1916."

A service was held on the lawn in front of the Ulster Tower just a few hundred yards from where George took those unforgettable photographs during the battle. After the service the veterans were given time to wander alone, or in small groups across the now peaceful slopes of the ridge. Some of them sought the graves of their old friends among the rows of headstones at Connaught and Mill Road cemeteries nearby. As George passed by each grave the roll call would have echoed in his mind as he read the names carved on the stones, Blair, Bothwell, Bustard, Devlin, Dobbin, Fitzsimmons, McCleery, whom he photographed snoring beside John Ewing, McIlroy, John Reid Moore, Arthur Morrow and Captain Charles Owen Slacke. A walk past these same graves today is an incredibly moving experience, especially when one knows something about the men who gave their lives. For George the experience would have been overwhelming as he recalled the characters, their jokes and banter, and their final moments of life. Later that day the party assembled again at the Memorial To The Missing where wreaths were laid in honour of those without graves. Again George may have passed his hand across the names carved on the mighty monument. If he searched for the name of his old chum Paul Pollock he would not have found it; his name was not added until 2013.

In 1959 remembrance was once again at the forefront of George's mind. As a now Senior Elder at St Enoch's he was asked to lay the foundation stone of the church's War Memorial Hall. The stone was laid on the 3 October 1959 and remains there today, surviving the destruction of the original church building. Shortly after this event, some time in 1960 a chance encounter with a remarkable man combined with the intense remembrance and reflection brought about by the pilgrimage changed the remaining years of George's life and led to him resigning from the Kirk Session and leaving the Presbyterian Church.

Charles 'Chuck' Robertson MacDonald was born on New Year's Eve, 1916, in South Africa. Charles' parents originally came from Ireland and they returned to Belfast with him in his infant years. Later Charles attended the Royal Belfast Academical Institution between 1929 and 1934 before joining the Northern Ireland Civil Service. In August 1939, just days before the outbreak of World War Two, Charles joined the Royal Air Force Volunteer Reserve and when war was declared he was quickly sent on initial training and then on to flying school. By November 1940 Chuck was flying operational sorties over France and Germany with Bomber Command as a Flight Sergeant in Armstrong Whitworth Whitley twin engined bombers. He transferred into various operational squadrons flying Halifax bombers before moving to No 90 Squadron where he was one of the first RAF pilots to fly the American Boeing B-17 Flying Fortress. By late 1941 he was commissioned as Flying Officer. He was later selected to travel to the United States where his combat experience was utilised in evaluating and developing the B-17 and Liberator bombers for combat use.

Chuck then spent a period instructing pilots on Halifax aircraft until he was promoted as Squadron Leader to No 78 Squadron. With 78 Squadron he took part in the first '1000 Bomber Raid' on Cologne in Germany when on the night of the 30/31 May 1942 over 2200 tons of bombs were dropped within a period of 50 minutes on the city, causing hundreds of casualties. The squadron also took part in the epic attack on the Peenemunde V2 rocket site on the night of the 17/18 August 1943. In September 1943 Chuck was awarded the Distinguished Flying Cross (DFC) and later, in October

1944 he was awarded the Distinguished Service Order (DSO) and was named in *Flight Magazine* as one of the four top Bomber Command 'Aces'. The citation for his DSO read:

> "Squadron Leader C R MacDonald DFC
> This officer has completed a very large number of sorties and has successfully bombed some of the most heavily defended targets in Germany. He has set the highest example of bravery and devotion to duty, which together with great skill, have inspired all. His record is worthy of the greatest praise."

In a photograph taken during his early service at Hastings in 1939 (right), Charles MacDonald can be seen, second from right, with four other trainee airmen. Of the five men in the photograph he was the only one to survive the war.

Charles MacDonald left the Royal Air Force at the end of the war having attained Wing Commander rank. He returned to Belfast with his wife Yvonne and rejoined the Northern Ireland Civil Service. Although the war had ended the violence and turmoil of what he had experienced did not leave him. He was frequently affected by nightmares as the ghosts of his past returned to him in the quiet hours. Apart from his taking part in the horrific raids on the German cities and the feelings of responsibility that he may have harboured for the deaths of those left in his wake, he also suffered the loss of many of his fellow aircrew. On numerous occasions he was required to identify the bodies of his men who were killed in the air and returned with their battered aircraft or who died after crash landings, so painfully close to returning alive. Charles' son Iain can recall touching on the subject during conversation with his father:

Courtesy of Iain MacDonald

"Well, I asked him about how he felt, and there were two things; one is that he expressed this kind of detachment from what's happening below; you're up there, you had a job to do, you were obviously, flak around you, but it wasn't something that you were thinking about, even if there were rings of fire below you, and no doubt all sorts of horrors… you were just somehow literally and metaphorically above it all. The other thing was also this notion about survival, is the sense that it wasn't going to be you. It would be, maybe, other people who were going to perish, or not come back, but it wasn't going to be you. As a boy, I was sort of intrigued by this notion."

Charles, at that time was not in any way a religious man but his son can recall that during the late 1950s he did perceive that his father may have been attempting to find some form of peace within himself. He attended church services along with his wife Yvonne, in an attempt to try to connect with a particular faith but none could give him what he was looking for. Then, one day Yvonne's parents were walking in Royal Avenue in Belfast when they happened upon a sign outside the Grand Central Hotel inviting members of the public to enter and join a Baha'i meeting inside. As a result of attending the meeting the couple joined the Baha'i's and later told Charles and Yvonne about it. Over a period of around six months Iain questioned and also read about the Baha'i teachings. Eventually, after meeting and questioning other Baha'is Charles and Yvonne became Baha'is themselves. Charles followed the teachings with a passion and used every opportunity to talk to others and tell them about it.

By 1960 Charles MacDonald was working in the Government Buildings at Stormont in Belfast. George Hackney was living at Dundonald nearby and was seeking new premises for his massage practice closer to his home and his sister's florist business where he frequently helped out. He noticed a house on his daily commute that was advertised 'To Let' at 75 Upper Newtownards Road. Over a period of time the house remained advertised for rental until one day the sign changed and it was placed on the market, for sale. He immediately bought the property and began running his business from it. Shortly afterwards Charles MacDonald noticed the practice, close to his work at Stormont and telephoned George to make an appointment for treatment for back pain that he was suffering. George had become increasingly popular and when he received the call from Charles his appointment book was full. Charles however was persistent and eventually George gave him an appointment at the end of the day. He later said that he had "listened to a voice in his head" and gave Charles the booking.

During the course of the treatment the two men realised that they had a common bond. They had both been exposed to horrific, unforgettable experiences carrying out two different roles in two very different wars a generation apart. They had both suffered in their own quiet ways, reluctant to betray their thoughts or share their past experiences with people who may not understand. In the confines and privacy of the small treatment room at 75 Upper Newtownards Road in Belfast these two men at once understood each other. Charles told George about the Baha'i faith and from that first meeting George set about discovering everything that he could about the religion.

For the next three years George attended meetings and asked questions. He recorded the answers on a reel to reel tape recorder that he owned and listened to the recordings again at home. From these recordings he formulated further questions which he again put to Baha'i's in subsequent meetings which were again recorded, and so the process went on until in 1963 George made the considered decision to resign from his position as Senior Elder in the Kirk Sessions of St Enoch's Presbyterian Church.

Bobby McClung was himself an Elder at that time and was present at the Kirk Session meeting when his resignation was tendered. The event was recorded in the Kirk Session minutes:

"Mr George N Hackney resigned from the active duties of the eldership. This, the session accepted with regret. Ordained in 1931, Mr Hackney has served faithfully on session and committee. Having the courage of his convictions, he was unafraid to express them in a Christian and courteous manner."

Bobby recalls:

"From what I can remember about this period, which, of course, was just my first year on the Kirk Session, that Mr Hackney was not attending the meetings as regularly as he must have been doing in the past, that he was gradually a vague figure, and it was obviously that his resignation was, perhaps, expected, at this stage, but accepted with regret. It was Mr Hackney's own decision that he was leaving the congregation, and perhaps to the Presbyterian Church, at this time."

We can ask the obvious question, why? Such questions, that touch on a person's inner beliefs and thoughts, although simple and perhaps obvious, nevertheless can cut deeply into the respondent's personal thoughts. One can wonder and guess and try to add reason based on our own lives but George had made up his mind after thorough consideration added to a lifetime of experiences, some of which he would rather, but never could forget. The decision was a personal one and it was not made in haste. The best explanation was given to the author by Bobby McClung himself who had the benefit of knowing George and gave a sympathetic and impartial explanation in the following terms:

"The journey of faith is a progression and you keep on that particular path; you don't reach your destination until the life hereafter. The journey is not an easy one. It's not easy in your early years, and it's not easy in your senior years. Myself, I have completed now 53 years as a ruling elder, and I'm still on a journey, and I still have to consider my own faith. If I was led to leave a congregation, if I felt I was being led to leave a particular congregation or faith, then I would have to do that. I would have to follow it, but it would be after much prayerful consideration. I have been very happy in the congregations in which I have served. I am very happy in the congregation that I am now in, but I think we all should examine ourselves and our faith, to see what is God's will for us.

I would believe that George, changing from one denomination to another, at that time of life, he didn't take it easily, that he must have considered it and prayed about it for perhaps a number of years, that it just was not an instant decision on his part, but it was something that had been preying on his mind, and he came to a decision and followed it."

Iain MacDonald, himself a Baha'i with fond memories of George gives us his own assessment, which remarkably follows a familiar line:

"Well, I think that here were two men who did reflect on life… My father was already a Baha'i, and it's not that you've got it all wrapped up and settled by any stretch of the imagination, because you've become a Baha'i, it's still a journey, it's still an investigation, but George obviously was somebody who was very alert or sensitive to new things, or certainly trying to get some answers to some of his questions. So here, these two men came together and they would inevitably be talking about social issues or things that were going on around them. So it wouldn't have taken very long, and certainly, for my dad to have explained his own perspective. And inevitably, obviously, George was alert to spiritual discussion. He was a man who was willing to have, I suppose, a spiritual conversation in a way that maybe other people might not have been. So I think they would have just found their way to that, and then that was it."

Another man who knew George in his latter years was Hushang Jamshidi, also a Baha'i. Hushang often met George at his home in Dundonald. He can recall that once the two men began discussing matters of faith George's wife Ella would leave the room and let them talk in peace. Ella remained a member of St Enoch's and George drove her to the church but remained outside the church in his car while she attended the services. This continued until Ella passed away in 1973.

One one occasion, while George was chatting in his house to Hushang he paused in the conversation and indicated that he had something he wanted Hushang to see. George went upstairs and returned with an album of photographs. He handed it to his friend who opened it and discovered the photographic record now reproduced within these pages. The photographs that he had taken showing the faces of ghosts from a distant dark past had followed him into a new age and remained with him to the end of his days. They could never be forgotten, immortalised in print.

Iain MacDonald, when he learnt of the photograph album commented:

"I knew about his experience, that he fought in the Somme, something he never talked about, [I] never knew about it [the album]. So when I heard about the photographs, it came as an absolutely extraordinary surprise... I mean, I didn't know George was a photographer; I really didn't... it was just extraordinary that George had actually made this unique contribution to history and that actually rather excites me and pleases me, because George had such extraordinary qualities, and for the most part, he was a man who lived his life without people being particularly aware of him."

George Naphtali Hackney passed away at the Ulster Hospital in Dundonald on the fourth of October 1977. All that he possessed was left to the National Spiritual Assembly of the Baha'i's of the United Kingdom along with strict instructions regarding his burial. In the knowledge that many of his old comrades were not afforded that simplest of dignities, his headstone, carved from a piece of Mourne granite, carries only the name 'Hackney' without any further dates or inscription. The simple headstone, in a strangely comforting way is a more than appropriate monument to mark the final resting place of the man we know him to have been. The man at one with nature. The warrior. The quiet unassuming gentleman. The man of faith seeking a oneness of Mankind and World Peace. Ulster's finest war photographer whose work remained locked away, unseen, along with his own bitter memories.

Opposite: Courtesy of
Iain MacDonald